COLLECTOR'S
VALUE GUIDE™

Dale Earnhardt®

Collector Handbook
and Price Guide

PREMIERE EDITION

DALE EARNHARDT®

This publication is not affiliated with Dale Earnhardt®, Dale Earnhardt Inc., Richard Childress Racing Enterprises Inc., General Motors Corporation, NASCAR® or any affiliates, subsidiaries, distributors or representatives. Any opinions expressed are solely those of the authors, and do not necessarily reflect those of Dale Earnhardt®, Dale Earnhardt Inc., Richard Childress Racing Enterprises Inc., General Motors Corporation or NASCAR®. Dale Earnhardt® is a registered trademark of Dale Earnhardt Inc. The likeness of the #3 race car, the stylized #3 and the RCR checkered flag logo design are trademarks of Richard Childress Racing Enterprises Inc. NASCAR® and the NASCAR® logo are registered trademarks of The National Association for Stock Car Auto Racing Inc.

EDITORIAL

Managing Editor:	Jeff Mahony
Associate Editors:	Melissa A. Bennett
	Jan Cronan
	Gia C. Manalio
	Paula Stuckart
Contributing Editor:	Mike Micciulla
Assistant Editors:	Heather N. Carreiro
	Jennifer Filipek
	Joan C. Wheal
Editorial Assistants:	Jennifer Abel
	Timothy R. Affleck
	Beth Hackett
	Christina M. Sette
	Steven Shinkaruk

WEB
(CollectorsQuest.com)

Web Reporter:	Samantha Bouffard
Web Graphic Designer:	Ryan Falis

R&D

R&D Specialist:	Priscilla Berthiaume
R&D Graphic Designer:	Angi Shearstone

ART

Creative Director:	Joe T. Nguyen
Assistant Art Director:	Lance Doyle
Senior Graphic Designers:	Susannah C. Judd
	David S. Maloney
	Carole Mattia-Slater
	David Ten Eyck
Graphic Designers:	Jennifer J. Bennett
	Sean-Ryan Dudley
	Kimberly Eastman
	Marla B. Gladstone
	Melani Gonzalez
	Caryn Johnson
	Jaime Josephiac
	James MacLeod
	Jeremy Maendel
	Chery-Ann Poudrier

PRODUCTION

Production Manager:	Scott Sierakowski
Product Development Manager:	Paul Rasid

Photo Credits: pgs. 5 & 6 – ©Reuters NewMedia Inc./CORBIS; pgs. 3 & 13 – ©Brian Smith/CORBIS OUTLINE.

ISBN 1-58598-071-4

CHECKERBEE™ and COLLECTOR'S VALUE GUIDE™ are trademarks of CheckerBee, Inc. Copyright © 2000 by CheckerBee, Inc. All rights reserved. No part of this book may be reproduced or transmitted in any form or by any means, electronic or mechanical, including photocopying, recording, or by any information storage or retrieval system, without the written permission of the publisher.

CheckerBee PUBLISHING
306 Industrial Park Road
Middletown, CT 06457
CollectorsQuest.com

Table Of Contents

©Brian Smith/CORBIS OUTLINE

COLLECTOR'S
VALUE GUIDE™

Other Products & Accessories, cont.

Welcome To The World Of Dale Earnhardt®

He's known as "The Intimidator," a nick-name earned on the NASCAR® racetracks early in his 25-year racing career. From his Rookie of the Year campaign in 1979 to his current quest for a record eighth championship, "The Man In Black's" achievements nearly defy description. For many fans, Dale Earnhardt® embodies everything a NASCAR driver should be – a combination of heart, charisma, professionalism and skill. It's this unique combination that has made Earnhardt fans clamor to be part of their hero's world – and turn Earnhardt collectibles into a multi-million-dollar industry.

©Reuters NewMedia Inc./CORBIS

The Collector's Value Guide™ brings the entire Dale Earnhardt phenomenon straight to you, including:

- Feature articles about Earnhardt's life, his family, the various teams he has raced for and the different cars he has driven.

- An in-depth look at Dale Earnhardt collectibles with full-color pho-tographs, manufacturer names, scales and up-to-date secondary mar-ket values.

- Fun and (sometimes) hard-to-find memorabilia, such as replica uni-forms, helmets, lighters, games and remote-controlled cars.

- Other exciting sections, including the top ten most valuable die-cast cars, tips about caring for your collection and an overview of how the secondary market works.

Whether you're a casual Dale Earnhardt fan or a devoted collector, the Collector's Value Guide™ has something for you!

Dale Earnhardt® Biography

©Reuters NewMedia Inc./CORBIS

For many racing fans, Dale Earnhardt is more than just a NASCAR driver – he is NASCAR racing. Earnhardt is regarded as one of the fiercest competitors in any sport. Respected and feared by his opponents and loved by race fans worldwide, Earnhardt has parlayed his unmatched driving skills, courage and relentless determination into seven Winston Cup Championships. But it's hardly been an easy road for the man known as "The Intimidator."

The Early Years

Born Ralph Dale Earnhardt on April 29, 1951 in rural Kannapolis, North Carolina, Earnhardt was the third of five children born to Ralph and Martha Earnhardt. The children growing up in the Earnhardt household spent time with their father in his garage behind the house, working on his race cars. Driving car #8, the elder Earnhardt competed on short tracks all over the Southeast, earning a reputation as one of the more talented drivers on the stock car race circuit during the 1950s and 1960s.

It was in and around his father's shop that "Young Dale," as he was then called, spent most of his childhood. As he grew older, he helped out by sweeping the garage floor. Eventually, his responsibilities around the shop increased as he continued to earn his father's trust. Earnhardt's dream of becoming a race car driver just like his father took root and flourished under his father's tutelage.

A Passion Becomes A Career

Earnhardt started to fulfill his racing passion during his teen years, spending time in his father's shop and drag racing with his friends. Racing cars became an obsession, which eventually caused Earnhardt to quit school when he was 16, a decision he later acknowledged as the only regret in his life. Despite his father's protests, Earnhardt was convinced that he could make a living by following his dream of racing cars.

It wasn't an easy road. Although he raced regularly in Kannapolis, Earnhardt was forced to work several odd jobs to help finance his hobby, including employment stints at a welding shop, an insulation company and a service station. By the time he was 18, he was racing full time, but his intense schedule only increased his financial woes. He was forced to borrow money on a regular basis to buy the parts and equipment necessary to keep his fledgling career rolling.

Two early marriages and divorces further strained Earnhardt's situation so that by the early 1970s, he was deep in debt. Although he was successful on the dirt track, was stuck in a career rut that seemed to be going in circles.

Life took another turn for the worse in 1973 when Earnhardt's father – and hero – suddenly died of a heart attack at the age of 44. Losing his beloved mentor devastated Earnhardt but also re-energized his drive to succeed on the racetrack.

On To The Winston Series

After racing in the Sportsman Division for a time, Earnhardt started his Winston Cup racing career in 1975 at Charlotte Motor Speedway. Owner Ed Negre's Dodge left much to be desired in terms of performance, and this was an inauspicious debut. Earnhardt finished just ahead of Richard Childress, a man who would play an important role in Earnhardt's future racing career.

Earnhardt made sporadic starts on the Winston Cup circuit over the next three years and eventually landed a job driving for owner Rod Osterlund. Finally, after all those years of struggle, Earnhardt had earned his first full-time Winston Cup ride. He was touted as a promising young driver, but no one could have predicted the mark he would leave on NASCAR racing in the following year – or in the years to come.

The Road To Success

Racing against such superstars as Richard Petty, Darrell Waltrip and Cale Yarborough might have intimidated a less confident driver, but not Earnhardt. He wasted little time making a name for himself in his 1979 rookie season, earning his first career win in the Southeastern 500 at Bristol (Tennessee) International Raceway.

Darrell Waltrip   Richard Petty

Earnhardt earned the first of four poles that year at Riverside (California) Speedway and by the end of the season, had started 29 races, had 11 top-five finishes, earned more than $250,000, finished seventh in point standings and won the Winston Cup Rookie of the Year award.

Finally, after all those years of hard work and sacrifice, he had arrived – but even greater thrills awaited Earnhardt in 1980. He jumped out of the gate quickly, taking an early lead in points, a position that he struggled to defend against such pros as Petty and Yarborough.

When the season ended, Earnhardt beat Yarborough by a 19-point margin, claiming his first Winston Cup Championship. It was the first time in NASCAR history that a driver won Rookie of the Year and the Winston Cup Championship in consecutive years.

Earnhardt's professional star was indeed rising. After his stunning victory in 1980, two important events occurred that would change Earnhardt's life and help pave his way to future success. The first was the reappearance of Childress, the man Earnhardt had beaten in his first Winston Cup race in 1975. The second was his marriage to North Carolina native Teresa Houston.

A Winning Combination

Between 1981 and 1983, Earnhardt joined a succession of fledgling teams with hopes of becoming a serious contender in the Winston Cup circuit. Finally, in 1984, he and Childress reunited and formed a winning combination that eventually resulted in six Winston Cup Championships.

Meanwhile, Earnhardt and Houston were married in 1982. The niece of NASCAR Grand National driver Tommy Houston, Teresa Houston had known Earnhardt since she was 16 and had grown up not far from his hometown. She helped bring stability and a sense of fulfillment to the family-conscious Earnhardt, who is candid about how important his wife has been to his success. Together, they spearhead Dale Earnhardt Inc. (DEI), a multi-million-dollar company that owns two Winston Cup racing teams, a Busch Series team and a Chevrolet dealership that sponsored Ernie Irvan's Winston Cup debut in 1987.

Throughout the 1980s, Earnhardt established himself as the premiere Winston Cup driver. He won consecutive Winston Cup Championships in 1986 and 1987, the latter fueled by an 11-win season that ranks as one of the best in NASCAR history.

Earnhardt again brought home the Winston Cup in 1990 and 1991, but 1992 handed Earnhardt a disappointing 12th-place finish. He made a comeback to repeat his championship run in 1993 and 1994, the last of which earned him his seventh Winston Cup Championship, an accomplishment equaled only by Petty.

In 1998, after several unsuccessful seasons, Earnhardt finally came home with his first Daytona 500 win. Past performances included running out of gas in 1986, blowing out a tire on the final lap in 1990 and a collision in 1997. Only one more NASCAR challenge remains for Earnhardt – a record-breaking eighth Winston Cup Championship.

A Thriving Team

One can only speculate how much longer Earnhardt will continue his reign of the Winston Cup circuit in his signature #3 Goodwrench Monte Carlo. He has earned the reputation as one of the greatest drivers in NASCAR history, a distinction that he has strived to achieve from the very beginning of his career.

In addition to his outstanding racing accomplishments, Earnhardt has also played an important role in the resurgence of NASCAR's popularity that began in the 1980s, not only in terms of attendance figures and television ratings but also in merchandising and collectibles. Through DEI, the Earnhardts bring excellence to their racing teams and to DEI's other business ventures.

And, of course, there is the new generation of NASCAR drivers that Earnhardt has inspired, including his own family. So far, three of his four children have tried their hand at racing, although only his two sons are currently active. Dale Earnhardt Jr., a Busch Grand National champion, made an impressive debut in the 2000 Winston Cup circuit, competing for Rookie of the Year honors.

But the torch has certainly not been passed yet. As long as there are races to be run and cups to be won, fans can count on Dale Earnhardt to continue to intimidate his opponents and set the standard for NASCAR drivers into the new millennium – and perhaps win that eighth championship along the way!

The Earnhardt Family Racers

With three generations of skilled drivers, the Earnhardt family has established its name as a noble one within the world of NASCAR.

Ralph Earnhardt

A Memorable Moment

Dale Earnhardt raced against his father only once, on a dirt track near Charlotte, North Carolina. The elder Earnhardt drove his car up behind his son's car and gently nudged it ahead of another car during the race. He then won the race while his son finished third.

The Earnhardt racing legacy began in the 1950s with Ralph Lee Earnhardt, who raced his #8 stock car during the early days of NASCAR. Winner of the 1956 Sportsman Championship, Earnhardt was born in 1928 and died suddenly in 1973, leaving his son, Dale, in the driver's seat as the Earnhardt racing patriarch.

Kerry Earnhardt

Kerry Dale Earnhardt was born in 1969 to Dale Earnhardt and his first wife. As a teenager, he played many sports in high school, but he always felt at home working trackside as a tire changer for a local race team. Since then, he's taken his interest and talents to the track to achieve his place in the Earnhardt racing dynasty. After competing in the Busch Series in 1999 (driving the #40 ChannelLock Chevrolet for Doug Taylor Motorsports), Earnhardt set his sights on the Winston Cup Series. He currently lives in North Carolina with his wife, Rene, and their three sons.

Kelley Earnhardt

Kelley King Earnhardt enjoyed a brief racing career driving #38 in the Late Model Stock Car Series. Although she competed against some of the best drivers, she gave up her number (a combination of her father's and grandfather's numbers) to support her family with her business expertise. Born in 1972, she is the first member of the family to earn a college degree, and has worked for Sports Image Inc. and Action Performance Company Inc.

Dale Earnhardt Jr.

Following in his grandfather's and father's "race tracks," Ralph Dale Earnhardt Jr. has been racing cars since 1991 and began his professional racing career in 1996 in the Busch Series. Born in 1974 to Dale Earnhardt and his second wife, "Little E" won the the Busch Series Championship in 1998. Now driving for Dale Earnhardt Inc., "Junior" entered the Winston Cup Series at the beginning of the 2000 season, establishing his own image and racing style.

Teresa Earnhardt

Often cited as one of the reasons for her husband's success on the racetrack and in business, Teresa Houston Earnhardt runs much of Dale Earnhardt Inc. and is always at her husband's side to celebrate each milestone of his career. The niece of NASCAR driver Tommy Houston, she grew up trackside and was familiar with the responsibilities of being part of a racing family at a young age. She also owned the Lowe's Foods Pontiac Grand Prix that her husband raced in a 1989 Busch Series race.

The History Of NASCAR®

Racing has been a part of American culture ever since the turn of the century when horseless carriages competed in short tests of speed over country roads. These racing trials eventually were held on oval tracks, and by the 1930s, the Southeast had became a racing mecca with competitions on the flat, sandy beaches of Daytona, Florida, and on the one-mile tracks in Atlanta and Charlotte, North Carolina.

The Birth Of Nascar

As the popularity of racing increased, local businessmen promoted and scheduled races, hired drivers and opened garages to train mechanics. Bill France, the future founder of NASCAR, bought a service station in Daytona where he raced on an oval beach-and-road course built in the mid-1930s. By the 1940s, the sport still had no standardized rules and France was concerned that racing would never get the recognition it needed to become more than a local or regional draw.

In 1946, France launched the National Championship Stock Car Circuit, which sponsored races all over the Southeast. After a year of operation, France and his associates offered a set of regulations, enforcement powers and point systems, and called their organization the National Association of Stock Car Auto Racing. NASCAR was born, with France as its first president.

Did You Know . . .

Some of the most successful early race-car drivers were moonshine runners from the Appalachians who drove modified cars designed for speed.

NASCAR sanctioned more than 50 races in its debut season in 1948. Its first race, a Modified event featuring older model cars, was held on February 15, 1948 at Daytona Beach.

On June 19, 1949, France staged NASCAR's first official Strictly Stock event with a $5,000 purse for the 150-mile race. Racing in new, showroom-quality cars was a completely new concept, one that France was certain would attract more spectators to the Charlotte Speedway. By the end of the season, Strictly Stock events had, indeed, become the country's premiere racing series and legitimized NASCAR's authority in the world of motorsports.

Pedal To The Metal: The 1950s & 1960s

In the 1950s, NASCAR racing began to change. The Strictly Stock series was renamed Grand National in 1950 and continued to be the preeminent racing division in the country. Dirt oval tracks were paved and new tracks were built. Then, in 1959, France opened his Daytona International Speedway, marking the first Daytona 500 and signaling the beginning of the large racetrack era.

Detroit's automobile manufacturers began competing for exclusive contracts with winning racecar drivers. By the late 1960s, industry-funded innovations such as larger engines and special performance vehicles pushed racing speeds to more than 200 mph, speeds that NASCAR officials considered

dangerous. These speeds prompted NASCAR to develop safety measures, including shoulder harnesses, roll cages and improved helmet designs.

Straightaway:
The 1970s & 1980s

In 1972, France retired as president of NASCAR and his son, Bill France Jr., took over to usher the country's fastest growing sports organization into an exciting new age. R.J. Reynolds Tobacco Company stepped in as a major sponsor of the sport in the early

1970s, the first corporate sponsor that did not produce automobile products. The series of races to win were now known as the NASCAR Winston Cup Grand National Series. The R.J. Reynolds contract included taped, televised national broadcasts of NASCAR races.

The first live broadcast of a major NASCAR event, the 1979 Daytona 500, featured a collision in the last lap, a surprise win by Richard Petty and a post-race fistfight. The broadcast became the talk of the nation and within a few years, cable and network television stations carried every Winston Cup race, completing NASCAR's transition from a regional draw to a national sport.

As a result of the media attention, the spotlight shifted from the cars to the drivers. Dynamic personalities such as Petty, David Pearson, Bobby Allison, Benny Parsons and Darrell Waltrip had to become both successful drivers and media-savvy public relations men who actively cultivated relationships with their fans. Petty ruled the speedways during the 1970s and became racing's most marketable star. But soon, this torch was passed to Dale Earnhardt, who made NASCAR history by winning the Winston Cup Series Rookie of the Year Award in 1979 and the Winston Cup Series Championship in 1980.

No Checkered Flag In Sight: The 1990s

Although the arrival of young, personable drivers during the early 1990s epitomized the new era of corporate auto racing, Earnhardt is still going strong in search of his eighth Winston Cup Championship. NASCAR's popularity reached an all-time high in the 1990s as the organization celebrated its 50th anniversary in 1998.

ABC Television network ratings for NASCAR events increased 62 percent during the decade as exhibition races were held for world-wide audiences. The 1990s also saw the creation of NASCAR's Craftsman Truck Series in response to the growing popularity of those vehicles on American roads.

2000 & Beyond

With multi-million-dollar purses, two new state-of-the-art race-tracks scheduled to open in 2001 (one in Joliet, Illinois, the other in Kansas City, Kansas) and official merchandise sales in excess of $1 billion, NASCAR racing seems poised for even greater heights.

Will "The Intimidator" earn that eighth Winston Cup Championship? How will advanced technology affect NASCAR racing? What does the future hold for the talented drivers of this fast-paced, action-packed sport?

The answers to these questions may quickly be answered as NASCAR races into the new millennium!

Inside NASCAR®

As with any other sport that has a devoted following, NASCAR has an array of terms and trivia that fans know. Here some of the basics to help you understand the ins and outs of stock car racing.

Proving Ground

The dream of every rookie driver is to compete in the Winston Cup Series, but this isn't the only way for drivers to find success on the tracks. Many drivers hone their skills in the Busch Series, which evolved in 1982 from the Late Model Sportsman Series. The Busch stock cars have shorter wheel bases and are slightly less powerful than their Winston counterparts; however, this doesn't mean that the Busch Series is any less competitive! It's hardly a step down from Winston - it's a step across.

Keep On Truckin'

If you love trucks, then the Craftsman Truck Series may be the very thing for you. In 1994, NASCAR officials realized that pickup trucks held racing potential. Now, such powerful pickups as Chevrolet Silverados, Dodge Rams and Ford F-150s compete at NASCAR tracks all over the country.

Size & Speed

The NASCAR tracks are just as diverse as the cars that race on them. Most people associate auto racing with the huge superspeedways at Daytona or Talladega, which are the largest with lap lengths of more than two miles. There are also two road courses on the NASCAR circuit (Sears Point Raceway and Watkins Glen International) that also range between two and three miles in length.

Intermediate tracks, such as Dover Downs International Speedway, are smaller, with laps of one to two miles each. Short tracks, such as Bristol Motor Speedway, are the smallest with laps of less than a mile. The shorter the track, the less room there is for drivers to accelerate to dangerous speeds.

Grand Old Flag

When drivers are hard at work, they do not want any distractions, but when there is something important happening on the track, they rely on the flagman to signal them with a series of colored flags. A green flag tells drivers when the race begins. A yellow caution flag tells the drivers to slow down because of an accident or debris on the track. If there's something wrong with the track, a red flag is raised, requiring all drivers to stop where they are.

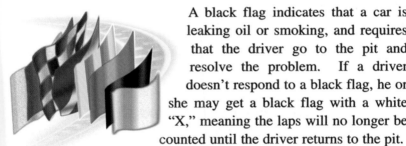 A black flag indicates that a car is leaking oil or smoking, and requires that the driver go to the pit and resolve the problem. If a driver doesn't respond to a black flag, he or she may get a black flag with a white "X," meaning the laps will no longer be counted until the driver returns to the pit.

As the race goes on, a driver might see a blue flag with a diagonal stripe. This means that the cars leading the lap are closing in and the driver should let them pass. A white flag means the driver in the lead is on the last lap, and a checkered flag means the race is over.

Dale Earnhardt®
Teams & Race Cars

For many of "The Intimidator's" fans, Dale Earnhardt and team owner Richard Childress are icons in the world of racing. With their GM Goodwrench sponsorship, they have become one of the most successful teams in NASCAR history. Earnhardt's #3 black Chevrolet Monte Carlo is easily one of the most respected vehicles on the track.

It wasn't always that way. Early on, Earnhardt struggled for team owners to notice him. It took years of racing before he found a corporate sponsor, and he wasn't always driving to Victory Lane in a Monte Carlo. Over the years, Earnhardt has paired up with a variety of sponsors, teams and cars before attaining his distinctive style.

A Ford Of A Different Color

The story of Dale Earnhardt's first stock car is legendary. The 1956 Ford Victoria originally had an apricot-colored roof and pink body, so Earnhardt's team decided to repaint the body of the car to match the roof. With no money to buy more paint, the team mixed the remaining paint together, but the entire car came out pink!

Years later, Action produced a die-cast car of the all-pink Ford. Dissatisfied with this version, Earnhardt prompted Action to produce a two-tone die-cast car with the original apricot top.

The Early Years

Earnhardt periodically raced old jalopies before he finally secured his first race car in 1969 when he was 18 years old. Earnhardt rebuilt the car – an old 1956 Ford owned by a neighbor, James Miller – and raced it at the Charlotte Motor Speedway in Concord, North Carolina, finishing in fifth place.

When Earnhardt started out on the Sportsman circuit in the early 1970s, his car bore #8 – his beloved father's number. He got his first taste of a Winston Cup race in 1975 at the World 600 at Charlotte, driving a 1975 Dodge owned by Ed Negre. Starting in 33rd place and coming in 22nd was not exactly a stellar beginning, but Earnhardt was determined to make a living racing cars.

During the 1970s, his sponsors included Hy-Gain and the Cardinal Tractor Company. He drove several makes and models, including a Dodge, a Chevrolet Malibu and a Chevrolet Monte Carlo. He was driving a Ford for Will Cronkrite in the 1978 World 600 when he first caught the attention of team owner Rod Osterlund.

One Tough Customer

A real-estate mogul from California, Osterlund had started a racing team and was actively seeking new talent. At the end of the 1978 season, Osterlund's number-one driver, Dave Marcis, left the team, leaving the driver's seat of the #2 Oldsmobile empty. Recognizing Earnhardt's potential, Osterlund asked Earnhardt to replace Marcis in 1979. With his first major team owner, Earnhardt was finally able to drive a better and newer class of cars.

The same success that led Earnhardt to his first Winston Cup Championship in 1980 also landed him his first major sponsor. Earnhardt's formidable driving style and cowboy image was perfectly suited for Wrangler Jeans®, and a partnership was formed that would finance his racing endeavor for nearly ten years. Earnhardt finished off the 1980 season at Ontario (California) Motor Speedway driving a blue and yellow #2 Dodge. The future looked bright. Earnhardt's new sponsor, however, couldn't relieve the problems beginning to plague Osterlund Racing. Turmoil over profits led Osterlund to sell the team to J.D. "Jim" Stacy in 1981.

Not For Sale

Earnhardt, however, didn't consent to the sale of his career. After driving a #2 Pontiac for Stacy for four races, he went to work for driver-turned-team owner Richard Childress. Using the #3 for the first time, Earnhardt kept the Wrangler sponsorship, but drove for Childress for only a few months. In debt, Childress could not finance a Winston Cup campaign and encouraged Earnhardt to find a new team. By the year's end, Earnhardt was driving for car builder Bud Moore.

Earnhardt spent two seasons racing a #15 Ford Thunderbird for Moore. Although impressed with Moore's ownership, Earnhardt did not have much success in the early 1980s. Then, in 1984, he left Bud Moore Engineering to rejoin Childress' team.

More Than One Wrangler

NASCAR fans might have been a little confused in 1984. When Earnhardt left Bud Moore's team to drive for Richard Childress, he took the Wrangler sponsorship with him, and Ricky Rudd took over Earnhardt's place with Moore. But Wrangler was still committed to both Moore and Earnhardt. So, the 1984 season saw two Wrangler cars on the race track – one for Earnhardt and one for Rudd!

That Winning Combination

Because of his experience as a driver, Childress was well-suited to NASCAR team ownership. By 1984, he had acquired more funds and put together a superior pit crew. Richard Childress Racing Enterprises Inc. was ready to begin its tenure as one of the best racing teams in the business.

The 1984 season opened with Earnhardt once again racing a #3 Monte Carlo at Daytona. His car sported a new paint scheme – a blue front with a yellow rear. But the colors did not show up well on the track so after that one race, the colors were changed back to the yellow front and blue rear.

Back In Black

Earnhardt brought the Wrangler sponsorship to Childress' team and continued the association until 1987 when his 11 wins attracted the attention of GM Goodwrench. Earnhardt's Chevrolets would thereafter take on the famous black paint scheme beloved by his fans – and feared by his rivals!

Model Citizen

Today, fans immediately recognize Earnhardt in his trademark black Monte Carlo, but this hasn't been the only model he has driven for Richard Childress Racing. During the early 1990s, Earnhardt briefly drove Luminas, and then, in 1995 at The Winston Select, he switched back to Monte Carlos. It was at this race that Earnhardt began a trend that was to influence other NASCAR drivers in the future – using special paint schemes on their cars. Earnhardt's Monte Carlo was painted all silver for The Winston to honor R.J. Reynolds' 25 years as a Winston Cup sponsor.

Let's Get Creative

Earnhardt was the first NASCAR driver to customize his cars with special paint schemes, and through the years, these schemes have increased in creativity. Despite his reputation as "The Man in Black," Earnhardt's 1996 car was given a patriotic look to commemorate the 1996 Olympics in Atlanta. In 1997, after becoming the first NASCAR driver to appear on a Wheaties box, his car for The Winston

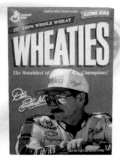

Select bore the cereal's orange color and logo. The next year, Earnhardt promoted one of his secondary sponsors, Bass Pro Shops, with a customized paint scheme.

Although Goodwrench remains his primary sponsor, Earnhardt has driven cars in special races and other countries that feature the colors of other companies. In November 1998, he drove a customized red Coca-Cola® Monte Carlo at the NASCAR Thunder Special Montegi Coca-Cola 500 in Japan. This was also the first time Earnhardt competed against his son, Dale Jr., who finished two places ahead.

The New Breed

Through years of valuable experience, Earnhardt has fought long and hard to gain his place of honor in stock car racing. After racing with a number of teams, sponsors and different car makes, he has settled into a winning combination of automotive performance, financial backing and driving expertise to make Richard Childress Racing one of the best known teams in NASCAR today.

Facts About The Tracks

Dale Earnhardt has traveled the country racing on Winston Cup circuit tracks, new and old. For 2000, there were 21 operating Winston Cup tracks, including two road courses, one rectangular track and a variety of oval tracks, all offering both fans and drivers a unique racing experience.

How are they unique? Both road courses on the schedule provide a race with more turns and intriguing topography than traditional oval tracks. Generally, tracks over a mile in length with high banking are considered superspeedways, while short tracks are less than a mile. In fact, the shortest Winston Cup track is only 0.526 miles long! No matter what the track design, "The Man In Black" has left his mark on all of them.

Atlanta Motor Speedway
Hampton, Georgia

Recently repaved and reconfigured, the Atlanta Motor Speedway is one of the fastest tracks on the Winston Cup circuit. The 1.5-mile quad-oval racetrack hosts two Winston Cup races per year and is often used in television commercials and movies.

FACT: Dale Earnhardt won his 75th Winston Cup race at Atlanta on March 12, 2000 at the Cracker Barrel 500.

Bristol Motor Speedway
Bristol, Tennessee

Known as "The World's Fastest Half Mile," the track at Bristol hosts two Winston races per season, including one of the Winston Cup's only night events. The half-mile track has 36-degree banking, the steepest of all NASCAR tracks.

FACT: Dale Earnhardt had his first Winston Cup victory at Bristol in April 1979 at the Southeastern 500.

California Speedway
Fontana, California

The California Speedway is one of NASCAR's newest tracks. In its four years of operation, the smooth two-mile, tri-oval has gained a reputation as being a favorite among drivers.

FACT: Dale Earnhardt was involved in a five-car accident at this track during the 1998 California 500. "The Intimidator" still finished ninth, a great feat considering he entered the race on a past champions provisional.

Darlington Raceway
Darlington, South Carolina

Drivers have been racing at Darlington since 1950. Considered the "Toughest Track to Tame" because of its egg-like shape and varied turn degrees, it's hard for driver's to leave the 1.3-mile track without a "Darlington Stripe" on their cars, the traditional sign of inadvertent wall contact.

FACT: On March 3, 1993, Dale Earnhardt set the Darlington speed record of 139.958 mph during the TransSouth Financial 500.

Daytona International Speedway
Daytona Beach, Florida

Home to numerous motorsports events throughout the year, Daytona International is NASCAR's most famous track. The 2.5-mile tri-oval hosts the Daytona 500, the Winston Cup's most renowned race.

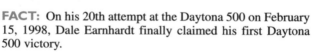

FACT: On his 20th attempt at the Daytona 500 on February 15, 1998, Dale Earnhardt finally claimed his first Daytona 500 victory.

Dover Downs International Speedway
Dover, Delaware

The "Monster Mile" is a cement oval with a lap of exactly one mile. Considered one of the most exciting tracks at which to watch a race north of the Carolinas, Dover Downs has run two Winston Cup races per year since 1971.

FACT: Dale Earnhardt won both races at Dover in 1989 – the Budweiser 500 and the Peak Performance 500. Oddly enough, Mark Martin took second and Ken Schrader came in third at both races.

Homestead Miami-Speedway
Miami, Florida

The inaugural Winston Cup Series race at this 1.5-mile Florida track was held in November 1999. Prior to 1999, the track was known primarily to the Craftsman Truck and Busch circuit races.

FACT: At his first race on the Miami track, Dale Earnhardt pulled up from the 23rd starting position to finish in the top 10.

Indianapolis Motor Speedway
Speedway, Indiana

Nicknamed "The Brickyard" because the track was originally brick-paved, Indianapolis became part of the Winston Cup circuit in 1994. Known best as the home of Indy car racing, Indianapolis's 2.5-mile rectangular track is home of the Brickyard 400.

FACT: Dale Earnhardt set the Brickyard's Winston Cup speed record (155.206 mph) on August 5, 1995.

Las Vegas Motor Speedway
Las Vegas, Nevada

This tri-oval 1.5-mile track located in the "Entertainment Capital Of The World" provides drivers with plenty of passing room, making for an enthralling race every year.

FACT: With his eighth place finish in the 1998 Las Vegas 400, Dale Earnhardt had the only Chevrolet to finish in the top 10 at Las Vegas' inaugural race.

Lowe's Motor Speedway
Concord, North Carolina

This North Carolina track hosts The Winston Select, NASCAR's all-star race held each May. Like the California Speedway, Lowe's is a favorite among drivers with its roomy 1.5-mile tri-oval track.

FACT: Dale Earnhardt's first Winston Cup career start was at Lowe's, then called Charlotte Motor Speedway, at the World 600 in 1975.

Martinsville Speedway
Martinsville, Virginia

The smallest (0.526 miles) and oldest (1955) track on the NASCAR race schedule, Martinsville was originally a dirt track and remains the perfect place to trade paint on a Sunday afternoon.

FACT: Dale Earnhardt won his first Martinsville race in September 1980, driving Rod Osterlund's #2 Chevrolet in the Old Dominion 500.

Michigan Speedway
Brooklyn, Michigan

Located near Detroit, the 2-mile Michigan Speedway has one of the widest laps in NASCAR racing. It's no surprise to see three and four cars racing abreast on the D-shaped oval.

FACT: Michigan's closest finish was recorded at the 1998 IROC race when Dale Earnhardt and Dale Earnhardt Jr. raced for the checkered flag.

New Hampshire International Speedway
Loudon, New Hampshire

Loudon, the only NASCAR racetrack in New England, hosts two Winston Cup races per year. The 1.5-mile track is similar to Martinsville and offers extreme racing through 12-degree turns and 5-degree straightaways.

FACT: In 1990, Dale Earnhardt qualified for pole position time just fractions of a second behind his son, Dale Jr., for the Jiffy Lube 300.

North Carolina Speedway
Rockingham, North Carolina

Otherwise known as "The Rock," this one-mile oval racetrack has traditionally hosted the second race of the Winston Cup season and is known for its rough surface, which inflates tire damage.

FACT: In 1993, Dale Earnhardt took second place to Rusty Wallace at Rockingham in both the GM Goodwrench 500 in February and the ACDelco 500 in October.

Phoenix International Raceway
Phoenix, Arizona

This D-shaped, one mile desert track is known for its complex turns and majestic surroundings. Since 1964, the raceway has been host to all divisions of racing.

FACT: Dale Earnhardt has had five top-5 finishes at Phoenix since it hosted its first Winston Cup Series race in 1988.

Pocono Raceway
Long Pond, Pennsylvania

Pocono Raceway is a superspeedway and road course all in one package. When preparing for a race at Pocono, drivers must build their cars to conquer tight turns and thrilling straightaways on the 2.5-mile triangle.

FACT: Dale Earnhardt won his first race at Pocono in the Summer 500 on July 19, 1987.

Richmond International Raceway
Richmond, Virginia

Racers and fans have frequented Richmond since its dirt track days in the 1940s. Redesigned to accommodate today's stock cars, the three-quarter-mile track is an enjoyable site for fans and drivers alike.

FACT: Dale Earnhardt swept the 1987 Richmond series, taking first place in both the Miller High Life 500 and the Wrangler Jeans Indigo 400.

Sears Point Raceway
Sonoma, California

Sears Point, one of two road courses on the Winston Cup circuit, is marked by hills and valleys unique to the Sonoma Valley raceway. The 11-turn course is almost two miles long and hosts one race per year.

FACT: Dale Earnhardt has recorded four top-five finishes since the track's first Winston Cup race in June 1989.

Talladega Superspeedway
Talladega, Alabama

Talladega is considered to be the fastest racetrack on the NASCAR circuit. Racers have set world speed records on this Alabama racetrack that stretches just more than 2.5 miles in length.

FACT: On July 28, 1996, a two-car collision sent 12 cars out of control, including Dale Earnhardt's car, which flipped onto its roof and skid down the track at 200 mph. Earnhardt walked away from the crash with only a fractured sternum and collarbone.

Texas Motor Speedway
Fort Worth, Texas

The second largest sports arena in the country, this quad-oval speedway runs 1.5 miles with 24-degree banking in the turns. With its resort-like amenities, fans flock to Fort Worth Speedway every year.

FACT: Dale Earnhardt has finished on average in approximately 16th place at his races at Texas Motor Speedway.

Watkins Glen International
Watkins Glen, New York

Known for its unusual right-hand turns, this upstate New York track has been host to many road-racing series. NASCAR held its first race here in 1957.

FACT: On August 9, 1996, Dale Earnhardt set the top qualifying time on the 2.45-mile road course with a speed of 120.733 mph.

Dale Earnhardt®
Collectibles

Thousands of fans flock to NASCAR races each week to see "The Intimidator," but the true extent of his popularity can be seen in the vast numbers of Dale Earnhardt-themed collectibles sold each year. On the retail level, the NASCAR collectibles industry is largely fueled by Earnhardt, Jeff Gordon and other popular drivers. On the secondary market level, Earnhardt is the undisputed king. This success comes from devoted Earnhardt fans and casual race fans alike. While there are many different types of collectibles devoted to "The Intimidator," a number of them stand head-and-shoulders over the rest.

Die-Cast Cars

The most popular Earnhardt collectibles are die-cast miniature replicas based on the actual cars Earnhardt has raced in the course of his 25-year career. These metal replicas typically feature hoods and trunks that open and front wheels that turn, and can be found with clear or black windows. Most often, particular paint schemes are reproduced in several different sizes. Die-cast cars are most frequently made in 1:24 and 1:64 scales, but collectors can also find 1:43, 1:32 and 1:18 versions of Earnhardt's most popular paint schemes.

Unlike other collectibles, which have both "open stock" and limited editions, the vast majority of die-cast cars are limited to a pre-determined production count. Very often, this count is indicated on the packaging or, for very special or extremely limited editions, is noted on a certificate of authenticity. This increases the collectibility and value of die-cast cars, particularly for popular or unusual paint schemes.

Some die-cast cars are available only through certain retailers or at special NASCAR events and become highly sought after for their limited distribution. Recently, the home shopping cable channel QVC offered exclusive Earnhardt die-cast cars that sold out within minutes.

Several manufacturers have produced Earnhardt die-cast cars over the years. Action Performance Companies Inc. is by far the largest die-cast manufacturer and has produced NASCAR collectibles for nearly a decade. In addition to standard die-cast offerings, Action also produces exclusive cars for its fan club, Racing Collectables Club of America Inc. (RCCA). Exclusive to club members, RCCA Elite editions come with black display boxes and certificates of authenticity that enhance their value.

Revell, another longtime die-cast manufacturer (now owned by Action), also offers general and collector's club editions. Brookfield Collector's Guild produces some of the more unusual die-cast items, such as 1:25-scale multiple car sets and Chevrolet Suburbans that feature Earnhardt's paint schemes. Other die-cast manufacturers include Racing Champions, Hasbro (Winner's Circle) and Ertl.

Other Collectibles

Some of the manufacturers listed above also offer 1:24-scale die-cast car banks. These look just like the 1:24 cars, but have a slot somewhere (usually on the trunk) into which collectors can drop their coins. Other, more unusual die-cast banks have been produced over the years, such as transporters, pit wagons and airplanes. Other items in this category are pewter and crystal cars, duallies and haulers.

Trading Cards

Now that NASCAR racing has established itself as a major sport, it's only natural that the NASCAR stars would be captured on sports trading cards. Before the recent trading card explosion in the early 1990s – led by Press Pass, Pinnacle, Upper Deck and other companies – there were only sporadic sports card issues, and these typically were packaged with  die-cast cars. Now, collectors can choose from hundreds of different cards depicting Earnhardt or one of his many race cars. Gold foil cards tend to be the most sought after, while other unusual items, such as special edition phone cards, have proven to be popular with many collectors.

Other Products & Accessories

 Although they are the most popular collectibles, die-cast cars and trading cards are only the tip of the Earnhardt collecting iceberg. Dozens of other memorabilia bearing "The Man in Black's" image and colors are hot-selling items throughout the country. These products include clothing, such as sweatshirts, T-shirts and even replica racing uniforms; toys, such as plush animals, electronic games and action figures; automobile accessories, such as mud flaps, bumper stickers and air fresheners; and a host of other collectibles, such as soda bottles, lighters, clocks and pocket knives. While most Dale Earnhardt fans are content to collect the die-cast vehicles, these other items have won the hearts of collectors as well. Whatever your taste, there's no shortage of Earnhardt collectibles to choose from!

Top Ten Die-Cast Cars

Over the years, many of the Dale Earnhardt die-cast cars have increased in secondary market value. These cars typically have been produced in low production runs, come detailed with 24K gold plating or commemorate an important event in Earnhardt's career. Following are today's ten most valuable die-cast cars, based on 2000 secondary market prices.

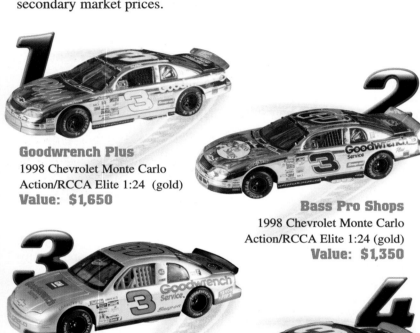

Goodwrench Plus
1998 Chevrolet Monte Carlo
Action/RCCA Elite 1:24 (gold)
Value: $1,650

Bass Pro Shops
1998 Chevrolet Monte Carlo
Action/RCCA Elite 1:24 (gold)
Value: $1,350

Winston Silver Select
1995 Chevrolet Monte Carlo
Action 1:24 (GM only)
Value: $975

Goodwrench Plus
1998 Chevrolet Monte Carlo
Action/RCCA Elite 1:24
(Canadian, LE100, gold)
Value: $900

Goodwrench
1988 Chevrolet Monte Carlo
Action/RCCA 1:24
Value: $625

Winston Silver Select
1995 Chevrolet Monte Carlo
Action 1:24 (GM Parts)
Value: $600

Wrangler
1987 Chevrolet Monte Carlo
Action 1:24
Value: $400

Goodwrench
1997 Chevrolet Monte Carlo
Action/RCCA 1:24 ("crash car")
Value: $350

Wrangler
1984 Chevrolet Monte Carlo
Action/RCCA 1:24
Value: $335

Wrangler
1981 Pontiac
Action 1:24
Value: $325

Anatomy Of A Race Car

Die-cast manufacturers take great care to accurately replicate Dale Earnhardt's stock cars, down to the smallest details. Here is an overview of some of the features found on the race cars.

1. Roof flaps – Flipped up, they keep a car from becoming airborne in a crash.

2. Rear spoiler – Adjusts to produce varying amounts of resistance.

3. Windshield – Made of Lexan™, the same material used for windshields on fighter jets.

4. Roll Cage - Steel tubing structure that surrounds the driver's area for protection.

5. Window net – Prevents the driver from being thrown out of the car.

6. Fuel cell – A 22-gallon gas tank lined with a rubber "bladder" to help prevent spills and fires in the event of a crash.

7. Tires – Treadless to provide more traction on the racetrack.

8. Exhaust – Pipes located under the driver's side window.

9. Lights – Headlights and brake lights are decals to avoid potential glass hazards.

10. Engine – Eight-cylinder engines, modified to produce significantly greater horsepower.

COLLECTOR'S
VALUE GUIDE™

How To Use Your Collector's Value Guide™

1. Locate your piece in the Value Guide. Die-cast cars are listed first, followed by other collectibles. All pieces are listed in chronological order by model year and include a listing of the manufacturers that have produced a version, as well as the scales available.

A red triangle (▲) indicates the manufacturer of the piece shown. (Note: There may be subtle variations between die-cast pieces produced by different manufacturers, so the car pictured may not be identical to the one in your collection.) Spaces are provided for you to write in limited edition (LE) information about each piece and to add other pieces or future releases. Trading cards, which begin on page 126, are listed in alphabetical order by manufacturer, then in chronological order by year. An alphabetical index begins on page 173.

2. Check off which versions you own next to the manufacturers' names. Record how many pieces you have in the "How Many" box. Add up the values for the pieces you own then record that amount in the "Total Value" box. "N/E" means the market value for that piece has not yet been established. Finally, add up all the quantities on each page and write them in the boxes at the bottom of each page.

3. Transfer the "Page Totals" to the "Total Value Of My Collection" worksheets, beginning on page 150. Add these totals together and you will have the grand total of your Earnhardt collection!

It's hard to believe that The Man in Black" began his racing career in a pink 1956 Ford Victoria. But when he was 18 years old, Dale Earnhardt's father suggested that he rebuild an old race car owned by a neighbor. Earnhardt worked nights and weekends to fix up the car then raced it at the Charlotte Motor Speedway in Concord, North Carolina, where he claimed fifth place. Finally, in a "real" race car instead of a jalopy, Earnhardt went on to win four more races in the Dayvault's K-2.

1

Pink Ford
1956 Ford Victoria

	Scale	LE	Value		Scale	LE	Value
☐ Action ▲	1:24		$88	☐ Action/RCCA Elite			
☐ Action	1:64		$24	(dark roof)	1:24		$75
☐ Action (dark roof)	1:64		$18	☐ Winner's Circle			
☐ Action/RCCA	1:24		$60	Lifetime Series	1:64		$11
☐ Action/RCCA	1:64		$35	☐			
☐ Action/RCCA (dark roof)	1:64		$18	☐			
☐ Action/RCCA Elite	1:24		$110	☐			

How Many: **Total Value:**   **Notes:**

Page Totals:	How Many	Total Value

COLLECTOR'S
VALUE GUIDE™

1975

Welcome to NASCAR! In May 1975, Dale Earnhardt made his first appearance in a Winston Cup race – and his first time running more than 200 laps. He completed 355 of the 400 laps at the World 600 at Charlotte Motor Speedway, driving a Dodge Charger owned by Ed Negre. Earnhardt finished in 22nd place, one position ahead of his future team owner, Richard Childress, and 45 laps down from the winner, Richard Petty.

1

RPM
1975 Dodge Charger

	Scale	LE	Value		Scale	LE	Value
❑ Action	1:24		$64	❑ Winner's Circle			
❑ Action ▲	1:64		$15	Lifetime Series	1:64		$23
❑ Action/RCCA	1:64		$14	❑			
❑ Action/RCCA Elite	1:24		$120	❑			

How Many: **Total Value:**   **Notes:**

1976

1

1976

Dale Earnhardt may have begun his racing career driving Fords and Dodges, but it wasn't long before he made his home behind the wheel of a Chevrolet. During the U.S. bicentennial year, Earnhardt raced two Malibus on the Winston Cup circuit. In November, he flipped his car several times during the Dixie 500 at the Atlanta Motor Speedway and, amazingly, came away with only a cut to his hand.

1

Army
1976 Chevrolet Malibu

	Scale	LE	Value		Scale	LE	Value
❑ Action ▲	1:24		$68	❑ Winner's Circle			
❑ Action	1:64		$15	Lifetime Series	1:64		$9
❑ Action/RCCA	1:64		$22	❑			
❑ Action/RCCA Elite	1:24		$135	❑			

How Many: **Total Value:**   **Notes:**

Page Totals:	How Many	Total Value

COLLECTOR'S
VALUE GUIDE™

Hy-Gain
1976 Chevrolet Malibu

	Scale	LE	Value		Scale	LE	Value
❑ Action ▲	1:24		$68	❑ Winner's Circle			
❑ Action	1:64		$15	Lifetime Series	1:64		$6
❑ Action/RCCA	1:64		$29	❑			
❑ Action/RCCA Elite	1:24		$155	❑			

How Many: **Total Value:**   **Notes:**

Driving a Ford Thunderbird owned by Will Cronkrite, Dale Earnhardt impressed team owner Rod Osterlund with a fourth-place finish at Atlanta in the summer of 1978. If Osterlund's driver, Willy T. Ribs, had shown up for practice that afternoon, Earnhardt may never have been asked to join Osterlund's team for 1979. Earnhardt ran a late-season race for Osterlund in an unsponsored Monte Carlo, a model that would become Earnhardt's trademark in years to come.

Rod Osterlund
1978 Chevrolet Monte Carlo

	Scale	LE	Value		Scale	LE	Value
❑ Winner's Circle				❑			
Lifetime Series ▲	1:64		$34	❑			
❑				❑			

How Many: Total Value: Notes:

Page Totals:	How Many	Total Value

COLLECTOR'S
VALUE GUIDE™

1979

When Rod Osterlund's number one driver, Dave Marcis, left the team, Dale Earnhardt (then a part-time driver) was put in the front seat of the Crane Cams Monte Carlo. He finished eighth in the Daytona 500, which was his first time racing at Daytona International Speedway. Earnhardt went on to celebrate his first Winston Cup career win in 1979 at the Southeastern 500 at Bristol Motor Speedway, and was named Rookie of the Year.

1

Crane Cams
1979 Chevrolet Monte Carlo

	Scale	LE	Value		Scale	LE	Value
❑ Winner's Circle				❑			
Lifetime Series ▲	1:64		$10	❑			
❑				❑			

How Many: **Total Value:**   **Notes:**

Page Totals:	How Many	Total Value

1980

2

1980

Dale Earnhardt was "one tough customer" driving the Mike Curb Wrangler, winning the Busch Clash at Daytona with his first corporate sponsor, Wrangler Jeans. He raced an Oldsmobile 442 on superspeedways and a Monte Carlo on short tracks. With five wins and 19 top-five finishes, Earnhardt captured his first Winston Cup Championship, becoming the first driver to win the Championship after being named Rookie of the Year.

1

Mike Curb
1980 Oldsmobile 442

	Scale	LE	Value			Scale	LE	Value
☐ Winner's Circle				☐				
Lifetime Series ▲	1:64		$34	☐				
☐				☐				

How Many: **Total Value:** **Notes:**

Page Totals:	How Many	Total Value

COLLECTOR'S
VALUE GUIDE™

2

Mike Curb
1980 Oldsmobile 442

	Scale	LE	Value			Scale	LE	Value
☐ Winner's Circle				☐				
Silver Series ▲	1:64		$16	☐				
☐				☐				

How Many:	Total Value:	Notes:

3

Mike Curb Wrangler
1980 Chevrolet Monte Carlo

	Scale	LE	Value			Scale	LE	Value
☐ Winner's Circle				☐				
Lifetime Series ▲	1:64		$10	☐				
☐				☐				

How Many:	Total Value:	Notes:

Page Totals:	How Many	Total Value

1981

Dale Earnhardt began the 1981 season with Osterlund Racing, but midway through the year, Rod Osterlund sold the team to J.D. "Jim" Stacy. After four races with this new team, Earnhardt left to join forces with Richard Childress. Facing financial troubles, Childress' team could not continue a Winston Cup campaign, so Earnhardt left the driver's seat of his first #3 Chevrolet Monte Carlo to race Ford Thunderbirds for Bud Moore Engineering for the remainder of the season.

1

Wrangler
1981 Pontiac

	Scale	LE	Value		Scale	LE	Value
❑ Action ▲	1:24		$325	❑			
❑ Action	1:64		$50	❑			
❑ Action/RCCA	1:64		$44	❑			
❑ Winner's Circle				❑			
Lifetime Series	1:64		$35	❑			

How Many: **Total Value:** **Notes:**

Page Totals:	How Many	Total Value

COLLECTOR'S VALUE GUIDE™

2

1981

Wrangler
1981 Pontiac

	Scale	LE	Value		Scale	LE	Value
❑ Action ▲	1:24		$295	❑			
❑ Action/RCCA	1:64		$50	❑			
❑				❑			

How Many: 1   Total Value: $295   Notes:

3

PHOTO
UNAVAILABLE

Wrangler
1981 Chevrolet Monte Carlo

	Scale	LE	Value		Scale	LE	Value
❑ Winner's Circle				❑			
Lifetime Series	1:64		$8	❑			
❑				❑			

How Many: Total Value: Notes:

1

1982

In 1982, Dale Earnhardt signed a two-year contract with Bud Moore Engineering and began racing Wrangler-sponsored Fords for the new team. He ended the season 12th in points, capturing one win for Moore's team. The victory came in the #15 Thunderbird at the CRC Chemicals Rebel 500 at Darlington in April – his first win in 39 races – and he celebrated the victory with his new wife, Teresa.

1

Wrangler
1982 Ford Thunderbird

	Scale	LE	Value		Scale	LE	Value
☐ Action	1:24		$130	☐			
☐ Action/RCCA ▲	1:24		$135	☐			
☐ Action/RCCA	1:64		$40	☐			
☐ Winner's Circle				☐			
Lifetime Series	1:64		$7	☐			

How Many: Total Value: Notes:

Page Totals:	How Many	Total Value

COLLECTOR'S
VALUE GUIDE™

1983

In his final year racing Fords for Bud Moore Engineering, Dale Earnhardt finished eighth in points, four slots ahead of his previous year's standing. He started in 30 races and was victorious in both the Busch Nashville 420 and the Talladega 500. Before joining Moore, Earnhardt promised Richard Childress that he would return to the team in the future. True to his word, he reunited with Childress once his contract with Moore expired at the end of the 1983 season.

1

Wrangler
1983 Ford Thunderbird

	Scale	LE	Value			Scale	LE	Value
❏ Action	1:24		$245	❏				
❏ Action/RCCA	1:64		$15	❏				
❏					▲ Pictured car is part of the Collector's Set.			

How Many: Total Value: Notes:

1984

Dale Earnhardt took two wins in 1984 and ended the season with 12 top-five finishes. He came in second at Daytona, driving his #3 Wrangler with its blue front and yellow rear. The car was repainted after the race, however, because the configuration of the light and dark paint was not easily visible on the track. Die-cast manufacturers recently reproduced a die-cast replica of this Daytona car to accompany Earnhardt's more recognized model.

1

Wrangler
1984 Chevrolet Monte Carlo

	Scale	LE	Value
❏ Action	1:64		$60
❏ Action/RCCA	1:24		$335
❏ Winner's Circle			
Lifetime Series (First Time)	1:64		$32

	Scale	LE	Value
❏ Winner's Circle			
Lifetime Series (Talladega)	1:64		$10
❏			

▲ Pictured car is part of the Collector's Set.

How Many: **Total Value:**   Notes:

Page Totals:	How Many	Total Value

Wrangler – Daytona 500
1984 Chevrolet Monte Carlo

	Scale	LE	Value		Scale	LE	Value
☐ Action/RCCA ▲	1:24		$205	☐			
☐				☐			

How Many: **Total Value:**   **Notes:**

1985

1

At the end of the 1984 season, the R.J. Reynolds Tobacco Company added an all-star race named The Winston Select. Reynolds also offered $1 million to the driver who won three out of four specific races – the Daytona 500, Winston 500, World 600 or Southern 600 – and named this The Winston Million. Although he did not win the Million, Dale Earnhardt did win four races in 1985, making the world of NASCAR stand up and take notice.

1

Wrangler
1985 Chevrolet Monte Carlo

	Scale	LE	Value			Scale	LE	Value
❑ Action ▲	1:24		$270	❑				
❑ Action/RCCA	1:64		$55	❑				
❑ Winner's Circle				❑				
Lifetime Series	1:64		$10	❑				

How Many: Total Value: Notes:

Page Totals:	How Many	Total Value

COLLECTOR'S
VALUE GUIDE™

PHOTO UNAVAILABLE

Wrangler
1985 Chevrolet Monte Carlo

	Scale	LE	Value		Scale	LE	Value
❑ Action (pewter)	1:64		$75	❑			
❑ Action/RCCA (pewter)	1:43		$50	❑			
❑				❑			

How Many: Total Value: Notes:

1985

1986

1

With NASCAR's popularity growing all over the country, Dale Earnhardt had 16 top-five finishes in his Wrangler Monte Carlo Fastback and won his second Winston Cup Championship in 1986. He also captured his second of six Busch Clash career wins. Earnhardt was named National Motorsports Driver of the Year and took home total winnings of $1.7 million, surpassing every Winston Cup driver that season.

1

Wrangler
1986 Chevrolet Monte Carlo

	Scale	LE	Value		Scale	LE	Value
❑ Winner's Circle				❑			
Lifetime Series (1997)	1:64		$28	❑			
❑ Winner's Circle				❑			
Lifetime Series (1999)	1:64		N/E	▲ Pictured car is part of the Collector's Set.			

How Many: **Total Value:**   Notes:

Page Totals:	How Many	Total Value

COLLECTOR'S
VALUE GUIDE™

1986

Wrangler
1986 Chevrolet Monte Carlo

	Scale	LE	Value		Scale	LE	Value
❑ Winner's Circle				❑			
Silver Series ▲	1:64		$13	❑			
❑				❑			

How Many: **Total Value:**   **Notes:**

1987

The 1987 season saw Dale Earnhardt solidify his place on the racetrack as NASCAR's "Intimidator." Victories at the first six races of the year made it clear to his opponents that the championship would once again be his. Earnhardt won his third Winston Cup Championshp and was named Driver of the Year by both American Motorsports and the National Motorsports Press Association.

1

Wrangler
1987 Chevrolet Monte Carlo

	Scale	LE	Value		Scale	LE	Value
❑ Action ▲	1:24		$400	❑ Winner's Circle			
❑ Action/RCCA	1:24		N/E	Lifetime Series (1999)	1:64		$9
❑ Action/RCCA	1:64		$60	❑			
❑ Winner's Circle				❑			
25th Anniversary	1:64		$10	❑			
❑ Winner's Circle				❑			
Lifetime Series (1998)	1:64		$12	❑			

How Many: Total Value: Notes:

Page Totals:	How Many	Total Value

Wrangler
1987 Chevrolet Monte Carlo

	Scale	LE	Value			Scale	LE	Value
☐ Action (pewter)	1:64		$75	☐				
☐ Action/RCCA (pewter)	1:43		$50	☐				
☐				☐				

How Many: | **Total Value:** | **Notes:**

3

Wrangler
1987 Chevrolet Monte Carlo

	Scale	LE	Value			Scale	LE	Value
☐ Winner's Circle Silver Series ▲	1:64		N/E	☐				
☐				☐				
				☐				

How Many: | **Total Value:** | **Notes:**

1988

Despite the introduction of carburetor restrictor-plates in NASCAR race cars, Earnhardt took 19 top-five finishes in the Winston Cup Series during the 1988 season. This proved to be an exciting year for die-cast fans. Earnhardt raced a Camaro in the American Speed Association (ASA) Series and a Monte Carlo fastback in the Busch Series. There are die-cast replicas of both the ASA Camaro and the Busch Grand National Monte Carlo.

1

Goodwrench
1988 Chevrolet Camaro

	Scale	LE	Value		Scale	LE	Value
☐ Action	1:64		$37	☐			
☐ Winner's Circle				☐			
Lifetime Series	1:64		$37	☐			

How Many: **Total Value:**   **Notes:**

Page Totals:	How Many	Total Value

COLLECTOR'S
VALUE GUIDE™

Goodwrench
1988 Chevrolet Monte Carlo

	Scale	LE	Value		Scale	LE	Value
❏ Action	1:64		$60	❏ Winner's Circle			
❏ Action/RCCA ▲	1:24		$625	Lifetime Series (Daytona)	1:64		$7
❏ Racing Champions	1:64		$33	❏			
❏ Winner's Circle				❏			
Lifetime Series	1:64		$20	❏			

How Many: **Total Value:**   **Notes:**

1989

Racing has always been a family sport, so it's no surprise that Dale Earnhardt raced the Lowe's Foods Pontiac Grand Prix owned by his wife, Teresa, in the Busch Grand National Series in 1989. That year, Earnhardt also battled for his third Winston Cup Championship, but he lost the Cup to Rusty Wallace by 12 points, which at the time was the narrowest margin in NASCAR history.

1

Goodwrench
1989 Chevrolet Lumina

	Scale	LE	Value			Scale	LE	Value
❑ Racing Champions	1:64		$170	❑				
❑ Winner's Circle				❑				
Lifetime Series ▲	1:64		$7	❑				

How Many: **Total Value:** Notes:

Page Totals:	How Many	Total Value

COLLECTOR'S
VALUE GUIDE™

PHOTO
UNAVAILABLE

Goodwrench
1989 Chevrolet Monte Carlo

	Scale	LE	Value		Scale	LE	Value
☐ Racing Champions	1:64		$58	☐			
☐				☐			

How Many:	Total Value:	Notes:

3

Lowe's Foods
1989 Pontiac Grand Prix

	Scale	LE	Value		Scale	LE	Value
☐ Action/RCCA	1:24		$128	☐			
☐ Winner's Circle				☐			
Lifetime Series	1:64		N/E	▲ Pictured car is part of the Collector's Set.			

How Many:	Total Value:	Notes:

1990

With a disapointing season behind him, Dale Earnhardt was in high gear at Daytona, leading on the last lap, when a tire blew on his Monte Carlo. Although he lost the race, he went on to win nine other races, claim his first International Race of Champions (IROC) Championship and finish in the top ten an impressive 23 times. He took home his fourth Winston Cup Championship and $3.3 million for the year.

1

Goodwrench
1990 Chevrolet Lumina

	Scale	LE	Value		Scale	LE	Value
❑ Matchbox/White Rose				❑ Winner's Circle			
Super Stars	1:64		$60	25th Anniversary	1:43		$18
❑ Racing Champions				❑ Winner's Circle			
(Goodwrench on trunk)	1:64		$280	Lifetime Series	1:64		$28
❑ Racing Champions				❑			
(Performance Parts)	1:64		$110	▲ Pictured car is part of the Collector's Set.			

How Many:	Total Value:	Notes:

Page Totals:	How Many	Total Value

COLLECTOR'S
VALUE GUIDE™

Goodwrench
1990 Chevrolet Lumina

	Scale	LE	Value			Scale	LE	Value
❑ Winner's Circle				❑				
Silver Series ▲	1:64		$20	❑				
❑				❑				

How Many: **Total Value:** **Notes:**

1991

Dale Earnhardt brought home 21 top-ten finishes and his fifth Winston Cup Championship in the 1991 season, proving that teamwork, dedication and determination make a winning combination. With two back-to-back championships to his credit, Earnhardt saw the beginning of an impressive decade in which "The Man In Black" would thrill the NASCAR world with a driver unlike any since the legendary Richard Petty.

Goodwrench
1991 Chevrolet Lumina

	Scale	LE	Value		Scale	LE	Value
❑ Matchbox (Quick Lube)	1:64		$40	❑ Racing Champions (Properties on stand)	1:64		$220
❑ Matchbox (Western Steer) ▲	1:64		$29	❑ Winner's Circle Lifetime Series	1:64		$8
❑ Racing Champions (Earnhardt Back)	1:64		$60	❑			
❑ Racing Champions (Petty Back)	1:64		$110	❑			
				❑			

How Many: **Total Value:** **Notes:**

Page Totals: **How Many** **Total Value**

COLLECTOR'S VALUE GUIDE™

Goodwrench
1991 Chevrolet Lumina

	Scale	LE	Value		Scale	LE	Value
❑ Winner's Circle				❑			
Silver Series ▲	1:64		$20	❑			
❑				❑			

How Many:	Total Value:	Notes:

Dale Earnhardt's Goodwrench team, led by new crew chief Andy Petree, spent much of 1992 trying to conquer the strains of staff reorganization. Although the racing season proved frustrating for Earnhardt and his crew with only one win (the Coca-Cola 600 in May), the new team adopted new strategies and returned to the winner's circle in 1993 with six wins.

1

Goodwrench
1992 Chevrolet Lumina

	Scale	LE	Value		Scale	LE	Value
❑ Ertl	1:18		$150	❑ Racing Champions			
❑ Matchbox/White Rose				(tampo printing)	1:24		$150
Super Stars (Mom 'n' Pops)	1:64		$12	❑ Racing Champions Premier	1:43		$40
❑ Matchbox/White Rose				❑ Racing Champions Premier	1:64		$40
Super Stars (no stripes) ▲	1:64		$15	❑			
❑ Racing Champions				❑			
(fender stickers)	1:24		$150	❑			

How Many: ___ Total Value: ___ Notes: ___

Page Totals:	How Many	Total Value

COLLECTOR'S
VALUE GUIDE™

In a NASCAR season struck by tragedy with the deaths of Davey Allison and Alan Kulwicki in aircraft accidents just three months apart, Dale Earnhardt turned in a stellar campaign with six wins, 17 top-five finishes and a record-setting speed of 139.958 mph at Darlington Speedway in November. He became the first three-time winner of The Winston at Lowe's Motor Speedway, then topped off the season with his sixth Winston Cup Championship.

1

Goodwrench
1993 Chevrolet Lumina

	Scale	LE	Value		Scale	LE	Value
❏ Racing Champions				❏ Revell (6-Time)	1:24		$40
(Mom 'n' Pops)	1:24		$80	❏ Revell/Sports Image	1:24		$30
❏ Racing Champions				❏ Winner's Circle			
(white fender)	1:24		$75	25th Anniversary Series	1:43		N/E
❏ Racing Champions				❏ Winner's Circle			
(yellow fender)	1:24		$75	Lifetime Series ▲	1:64		$8
❏ Racing Champions	1:43		$30	❏			
❏ Racing Champions	1:64		$25	❏			
❏ Racing Champions Premier	1:43		$80	❏			

How Many: **Total Value:**   **Notes:**

Page Totals:	How Many	Total Value

2

Goodwrench
1993 Chevrolet Lumina

	Scale	LE	Value			Scale	LE	Value
❑ Matchbox/White Rose				❑				
Super Stars ▲	1:64		$40	❑				
❑				❑				

How Many: | **Total Value:** | **Notes:**

3

Goodwrench
1993 Chevrolet Lumina

	Scale	LE	Value			Scale	LE	Value
❑ Winner's Circle				❑				
Silver Series ▲	1:64		$18	❑				
❑				❑				

How Many: | **Total Value:** | **Notes:**

Page Totals:	How Many	Total Value

Dale Earnhardt captured his seventh Winston Cup Championship in 1994, tying Richard Petty's record. With four first-place wins and 19 top-five finishes, Earnhardt earned many honors, including being named National Motorsport Driver of the Year and American Motorsport Driver of the Year. He also became the first Winston Cup driver to appear on "The Tonight Show" with Jay Leno, where they raced tractors around the studio lot. Earnhardt, of course, won!

1

Goodwrench
1994 Chevrolet Lumina

	Scale	LE	Value		Scale	LE	Value
❑ Action	1:64		$40	❑ Racing Champions Premier			
❑ Action/RCCA ▲	1:24		$350	(Brickyard 400)	1:64		$55
❑ Action/RCCA	1:64		$30	❑ Revell	1:24		$30
❑ Matchbox/White Rose				❑ Winner's Circle			
Super Stars	1:64		$15	Lifetime Series	1:64		$8
❑ Racing Champions Premier	1:43		$60	❑			
❑ Racing Champions Premier	1:64		$12	❑			

How Many: **Total Value:**   **Notes:**

Page Totals:	How Many	Total Value

2

Goodwrench
1994 Chevrolet Lumina

	Scale	LE	Value		Scale	LE	Value
❑ Winner's Circle				❑			
Silver Series ▲	1:64		$9	❑			
❑				❑			

How Many: **Total Value:**   **Notes:**

3

**PHOTO
UNAVAILABLE**

Goodwrench – Busch Series
1994 Chevrolet Lumina

	Scale	LE	Value		Scale	LE	Value
❑ Action	1:64		$25	❑			
❑ Action/RCCA	1:64		$48	❑			
❑ Sports Image (Kellogg's)	1:24		N/E	❑			

How Many: **Total Value:**   **Notes:**

Page Totals:	How Many	Total Value

COLLECTOR'S
VALUE GUIDE™

This was a landmark year for race fans and die-cast lovers alike. Dale Earnhardt not only won his second International Race of Champions (IROC) Championship, but he also became the "Man In Silver" at The Winston Select, driving a silver car to celebrate R.J. Reynolds Tobacco Company's 25th anniversary in NASCAR racing. He also drove a test car at Daytona to determine the final configuration of the new Chevrolet body style, which die-cast manufacturers replicated.

1

Goodwrench
1995 Chevrolet Monte Carlo

	Scale	LE	Value		Scale	LE	Value
☐ Action	1:24		$135	☐ Ertl	1:18		$75
☐ Action	1:64		N/E	☐ Matchbox/White Rose			
☐ Action/RCCA (w/headlights)	1:24		$250	Super Stars	1:64		$8
☐ Action/RCCA				☐ Matchbox/White Rose			
(w/out headlights) ▲	1:24		$285	Super Stars (7-time champ)	1:64		$45
☐ Action/RCCA	1:64		N/E	☐			
☐ Action/RCCA				☐			
(black window)	1:64		$38	☐			

How Many: | **Total Value:** | **Notes:**

2

Goodwrench
1995 Chevrolet Monte Carlo

	Scale	LE	Value		Scale	LE	Value
❏ Action (pewter)	1:64		$50	❏			
❏ Action/RCCA (pewter) ▲	1:43		$85	❏			
❏				❏			

How Many: **Total Value:**   **Notes:**

3

Goodwrench – Brickyard 400
1995 Chevrolet Monte Carlo

	Scale	LE	Value		Scale	LE	Value
❏ Action ▲	1:24		$110	❏			
❏ Action (w/card)	1:24		$140	❏			
❏ Action	1:64		$23	❏			
❏ Winner's Circle				❏			
Lifetime Series	1:64		$8	❏			

How Many: **Total Value:**   **Notes:**

Page Totals:	How Many	Total Value

COLLECTOR'S
VALUE GUIDE™

4

Winston Silver Select
1995 Chevrolet Monte Carlo

	Scale	LE	Value		Scale	LE	Value
❑ Action	1:18		$125	❑ Brookfield	1:25		$200
❑ Action ▲	1:24		$975	❑ Ertl	1:18		$175
❑ Action	1:32		$70	❑ Winner's Circle	1:24		$38
❑ Action	1:64		$85	❑ Winner's Circle			
❑ Action (GM Parts)	1:64		$600	Lifetime Series	1:64		$40
❑ Action (LE-20,000)	1:64		N/E	❑			
❑ Action (promo blister pack)	1:64		$85	❑			
❑ Action/RCCA	1:64		$130	❑			
❑ Action/RCCA Elite	1:24		$270				

How Many:	Total Value:	Notes:

5

Winston Silver Select
1995 Chevrolet Monte Carlo

	Scale	LE	Value		Scale	LE	Value
❑ Action/RCCA (pewter) ▲	1:43		N/E	❑			
❑				❑			

How Many:	Total Value:	Notes:

Page Totals:	How Many	Total Value

1996

Dale Earnhardt again met frustration at the Daytona 500, missing a first place finish by 0.12 seconds behind Dale Jarrett. Although Earnhardt only won one race in 1996, it still was a memorable year. He drove his Chevrolet Monte Carlo at The Winston with a patriotic paint scheme in honor of the 1996 Olympic Games that were held in Atlanta. Then in August, he set a qualifying race record at Watkins Glen International with a speed of 120.733 mph.

1

ACDelco
1996 Chevrolet Monte Carlo

	Scale	LE	Value		Scale	LE	Value
❑ Action	1:24		$52	❑ Winner's Circle	1:24		$30
❑ Action (1996) ▲	1:64		$19	❑ Winner's Circle			
❑ Action (1997)	1:64		$15	Lifetime Series	1:64		$75
❑ Action (1997, hood open)	1:64		$20	❑			
❑ Action/RCCA	1:24		$95	❑			
❑ Action/RCCA	1:64		$38	❑			
❑ Brookfield	1:25		N/E	❑			

How Many: **Total Value:**   Notes:

Page Totals: | **How Many** | **Total Value**

COLLECTOR'S
VALUE GUIDE™

Goodwrench
1996 Chevrolet Monte Carlo

	Scale	LE	Value		Scale	LE	Value
☐ Action ▲	1:64		$15	☐			
☐ Action/RCCA	1:64		$26	☐			
☐ Revell	1:64		$10	☐			

How Many: **Total Value:** **Notes:**

3

Olympics
1996 Chevrolet Monte Carlo

	Scale	LE	Value		Scale	LE	Value
☐ Action	1:24		$55	☐ Revell	1:24		$28
☐ Action (Food City)	1:24		$115	☐ Revell	1:64		$30
☐ Action (Goodwrench box)	1:24		$100	☐ Revell Collection	1:24		$60
☐ Action (green box)	1:24		$150	☐ Winner's Circle	1:43		$17
☐ Action (Mom 'n' Pops)	1:24		$100	☐ Winner's Circle			
☐ Action ▲	1:64		$24	Lifetime Series	1:64		$13
☐ Action (black window)	1:64		$20	☐			
☐ Action/RCCA	1:64		$55	☐			
☐ Action/Sports Image	1:24		$75	☐			

How Many: **Total Value:** **Notes:**

1997

In 1997, Dale Earnhardt became the first race car driver to appear on a Wheaties cereal box, and raced a specially-painted orange Wheaties car at The Winston. Then, in a battle for the lead at Talladega in July, his Monte Carlo crashed into the wall and flipped onto its side. Despite a fractured collarbone, Earnhardt restarted his car and finished the race. Die-cast manufacturers produced a replica "crash car" to commemorate Earnhardt's determination and bravery.

1

ACDelco
1997 Chevrolet Monte Carlo

	Scale	LE	Value		Scale	LE	Value
❑ Action/RCCA Elite ▲	1:24		$85	❑			
❑				❑			

How Many: **Total Value:** **Notes:**

Page Totals:	How Many	Total Value

COLLECTOR'S
VALUE GUIDE™

2

Goodwrench
1997 Chevrolet Monte Carlo

	Scale	LE	Value		Scale	LE	Value
☐ Action	1:64		$27	☐ Winner's Circle			
☐ Action/RCCA	1:24		$220	Lifetime Series	1:64		$40
☐ Action/RCCA	1:64		$30	☐			
☐ Action/RCCA Elite ▲	1:24		$435	☐			
☐ Winner's Circle	1:24		$35	☐			
☐ Winner's Circle	1:64		$13	☐			

How Many: **Total Value:** **Notes:**

3

Goodwrench
1997 Chevrolet Monte Carlo

	Scale	LE	Value		Scale	LE	Value
☐ Action/RCCA				☐			
("crash car") ▲	1:24		$350	☐			
☐ Action/RCCA ("crash car")	1:64		N/E	☐			

How Many: **Total Value:** **Notes:**

1997

4

Goodwrench Plus
1997 Chevrolet Monte Carlo

	Scale	LE	Value
☐ Action	1:24		$80
☐ Action (Parts Plus)	1:24		N/E
☐ Action	1:64		$20
☐ Action/RCCA	1:64		$40
☐ Action/RCCA Elite ▲	1:24		$135

	Scale	LE	Value
☐ Winner's Circle	1:24		$13
☐ Winner's Circle	1:64		N/E
☐			
☐			
☐			

How Many:　**Total Value:**　**Notes:**

5

PHOTO UNAVAILABLE

Goodwrench Plus – Brickyard 400
1997 Chevrolet Monte Carlo

	Scale	LE	Value
☐ Action	1:24		$85
☐ Action	1:64		$25
☐			

	Scale	LE	Value
☐			
☐			

How Many:　**Total Value:**　**Notes:**

Page Totals:	How Many	Total Value

6

Wheaties
1997 Chevrolet Monte Carlo

	Scale	LE	Value
❏ Action	1:18		$120
❏ Action ▲	1:24		$185
❏ Action (mail-in)	1:24		$70
❏ Action (Snap-On)	1:24		$200
❏ Action	1:64		$35
❏ Action/RCCA	1:64		$65
❏ Action/RCCA (black windows)	1:64		N/E
❏ Action/RCCA Elite (gold number)	1:24		$335

	Scale	LE	Value
❏ Action/RCCA Elite (second run)	1:24		$200
❏ Action/Sports Image	1:24		$90
❏ Revell Collection	1:18		$195
❏ Winner's Circle	1:24		$20
❏ Winner's Circle Lifetime Series	1:24		$30
❏			
❏			
❏			

How Many: **Total Value:** $200 **Notes:**

1998

Dale Earnhardt finally wins at Daytona! On his 20th career attempt at the Daytona 500, Earnhardt not only took the trophy but set the third fastest time at the Daytona Speedway (averaging 172.712 mph) and became the first Daytona winner to take a purse of more than $1 million. In May, Earnhardt raced in The Winston with his Monte Carlo decked out in the colors and design of Bass Pro Shops – a nice fit for one of Earnhardt's favorite off-track hobbies, fishing.

1

Bass Pro Shops
1998 Chevrolet Monte Carlo

	Scale	LE	Value		Scale	LE	Value
❑ Action	1:18		$135	❑ Revell Collection Club	1:24		$125
❑ Action	1:24		$125	❑ Revell Hobby Select	1:24		$40
❑ Action	1:32		$50	❑ Revell Hobby Select	1:64		$28
❑ Action	1:64		$23	❑ Winner's Circle	1:24		$30
❑ Action/RCCA	1:64		$45	❑ Winner's Circle	1:43		$16
❑ Action/RCCA Elite ▲	1:24		$200	❑ Winner's Circle			
❑ Revell Collection	1:18		$100	Lifetime Series	1:64		$7
❑ Revell Collection	1:24		$90	❑			
❑ Revell Collection	1:43		$60	❑			
❑ Revell Collection Club	1:18		$215	❑			

How Many: **Total Value:**   **Notes:**

Page Totals:	How Many	Total Value
	1	$200

COLLECTOR'S
VALUE GUIDE™

Bass Pro Shops
1998 Chevrolet Monte Carlo

	Scale	LE	Value		Scale	LE	Value
☐ Action/RCCA (gold) ▲	1:32		$85	☐			
☐ Action/RCCA Elite (gold)	1:24		$1,350	☐			
☐				☐			

How Many: Total Value: Notes:

3

Coca-Cola
1998 Chevrolet Monte Carlo

	Scale	LE	Value		Scale	LE	Value
☐ Action	1:18		$100	☐ Revell Collection	1:64		$23
☐ Action	1:24		$55	☐ Revell Collection Club	1:18		$160
☐ Action	1:64		$18	☐ Revell Collection Club	1:24		$110
☐ Action/RCCA	1:64		$30	☐ Winner's Circle	1:24		$14
☐ Action/RCCA Elite ▲	1:24		$185	☐ Winner's Circle	1:64		$11
☐ Revell Collection	1:18		$115	☐			
☐ Revell Collection	1:24		$72	☐			
☐ Revell Collection	1:43		$36	☐			

How Many: Total Value: Notes:

COLLECTOR'S VALUE GUIDE™

Page Totals:	How Many	Total Value
	1	$100

4

1998

Goodwrench Plus
1998 Chevrolet Monte Carlo

	Scale	LE	Value
❑ Action ▲	1:24		$74
❑ Action	1:64		$14
❑ Action (hood open)	1:64		$13
❑ Action/RCCA	1:64		$25
❑ Action/RCCA Elite	1:24		$125
❑ Revell Collection	1:18		$120
❑ Revell Collection	1:24		$65
❑ Revell Collection	1:43		$40
❑ Revell Collection	1:64		$16
❑ Revell Collection Club	1:24		$140
❑ Revell Hobby Select	1:24		$40

	Scale	LE	Value
❑ Winner's Circle	1:24		N/E
❑ Winner's Circle Preview	1:24		N/E
❑ Winner's Circle Preview	1:64		$8
❑ Winner's Circle (Toys"R"Us)	1:64		$9
❑ Winner's Circle Lifetime Series	1:64		$8
❑			
❑			
❑			

How Many: **Total Value:** **Notes:**

5

Goodwrench Plus
1998 Chevrolet Monte Carlo

	Scale	LE	Value
❑ Action ▲	1:24		N/E
❑ Action/RCCA Elite	1:24		$1,650
❑ Action/RCCA Elite (Canadian)	1:24		$900

	Scale	LE	Value
❑			
❑			
❑			
❑			

How Many: **Total Value:** **Notes:**

Page Totals:	How Many	Total Value

COLLECTOR'S
VALUE GUIDE™

6

Goodwrench Plus – Brickyard 400
1998 Chevrolet Monte Carlo

	Scale	LE	Value		Scale	LE	Value
❑ Revell Collection ▲	1:24		$65	❑			
❑ Revell Collection	1:64		$13	❑			
❑				❑			

How Many: Total Value: Notes:

7

Goodwrench Plus – Daytona 500
1998 Chevrolet Monte Carlo

	Scale	LE	Value		Scale	LE	Value
❑ Action	1:18		$105	❑ Winner's Circle	1:24		N/E
❑ Action	1:24		$75	❑ Winner's Circle	1:43		$15
❑ Action	1:32		$48	❑ Winner's Circle	1:64		N/E
❑ Action	1:64		$19	❑ Winner's Circle			
❑ Action/RCCA Elite ▲	1:24		$150	Lifetime Series	1:64		$8
❑ Revell Collection	1:24		$70	❑			
❑ Revell Collection Club	1:18		$150	❑			
❑ Revell Collection Club	1:24		$70	❑			
❑ Revell Hobby Select	1:24		$40	❑			

How Many: Total Value: Notes:

1999

In 1999, Dale Earnhardt conquered the 2.66-mile Talladega Raceway for the eighth time. Despite a back injury, he ended the century seventh in point standings and won his third International Race of Champions (IROC) Championship. For die-cast collectors, the century's last year was full of surprises. Earnhardt returned to his old Wrangler colors for The Winston then commemorated the "Last Lap of the Century" in November with a special metallic paint scheme.

1

Goodwrench Plus
1999 Chevrolet Monte Carlo

	Scale	LE	Value		Scale	LE	Value
☐ Action	1:18		$85	☐ Winner's Circle			
☐ Action	1:24		$65	Pro Series	1:64		N/E
☐ Action/RCCA	1:64		$20	☐ Winner's Circle			
☐ Action/RCCA Elite ▲	1:24		$155	Speedweeks	1:43		$11
☐ Revell Collection	1:18		$100	☐ Winner's Circle			
☐ Revell Collection	1:24		$65	Speedweeks	1:64		$6
☐ Revell Collection	1:43		$30	☐ Winner's Circle			
☐ Revell Collection	1:64		$12	Tech Series	1:64		$12
☐ Revell Collection Club	1:18		$135	☐ Winner's Circle			
☐ Revell Collection Club	1:24		$110	Tech Series (Select)	1:64		N/E
☐ Winner's Circle	1:43		N/E	☐			
☐ Winner's Circle				☐			
Lifetime Series	1:64		$8	☐			

How Many: **Total Value:** **Notes:**

Page Totals:	How Many	Total Value

COLLECTOR'S VALUE GUIDE™

2

1999

Goodwrench Plus
1999 Chevrolet Monte Carlo

	Scale	LE	Value		Scale	LE	Value
❏ Winner's Circle				❏			
(Wal-Mart, gold)	1:43		N/E	❏			
❏ Winner's Circle (gold) ▲	1:64		$24	❏			

How Many: **Total Value:**   **Notes:**

3

Goodwrench Plus – 25th Anniversary
1999 Chevrolet Monte Carlo

	Scale	LE	Value		Scale	LE	Value
❏ Action	1:18		$90	❏ Revell Collection	1:64		$15
❏ Action	1:24		$60	❏ Revell Collection Club	1:18		$120
❏ Action	1:64		$15	❏ Revell Collection Club	1:24		$70
❏ Action/RCCA	1:64		$25	❏			
❏ Action/RCCA Elite ▲	1:24		$140	❏			
❏ Revell Collection	1:18		$75	❏			
❏ Revell Collection	1:24		$60	❏			

How Many: **Total Value:**   **Notes:**

1999

4

Goodwrench Plus – Last Lap
1999 Chevrolet Monte Carlo

	Scale	LE	Value		Scale	LE	Value
☐ Action ▲	1:24		$85	☐			
☐ Action	1:64		$16	☐			
☐ Action/RCCA	1:64		$35	☐			
☐ Action/RCCA Elite	1:24		$180	☐			

How Many: **Total Value:**   **Notes:**

5

Goodwrench Plus – Sign Car
1999 Chevrolet Monte Carlo

	Scale	LE	Value		Scale	LE	Value
☐ Action	1:18		$95	☐ Revell Collection	1:24		$50
☐ Action ▲	1:24		$55	☐			
☐ Action (QVC, Brickyard)	1:32		N/E	☐			
☐ Action	1:64		$12	☐			

How Many: **Total Value:**   **Notes:**

Page Totals:	How Many	Total Value

Wrangler Colors
1999 Chevrolet Monte Carlo

	Scale	LE	Value		Scale	LE	Value
❏ Action	1:18		$100	❏ Revell Collection	1:64		$16
❏ Action ▲	1:24		$70	❏ Revell Collection Club	1:18		$120
❏ Action	1:64		$16	❏ Revell Collection Club	1:24		$120
❏ Action/RCCA	1:32		$54	❏ Winner's Circle	1:43		$12
❏ Action/RCCA	1:64		$35	❏ Winner's Circle			
❏ Action/RCCA Elite	1:24		$200	Lifetime Series	1:64		$7
❏ Revell Collection	1:18		$100	❏			
❏ Revell Collection	1:24		$60	❏			
❏ Revell Collection	1:43		$38	❏			

How Many: 1   **Total Value:** $100   **Notes:**

2000

Line up all of Dale Earnhardt's 2000 Monte Carlos and one thing is clear – the racing machines carry a bold streak of colors that compliment his intimidating speed. Racing the Tazmanian Devil in the Daytona 500, then Peter Max's psychedelic design in The Winston, he propelled his racing career to new visual heights. The dawn of the new century saw Earnhardt capture his 75th career win, and in August, he won his fourth International Race of Champions (IROC) Championship.

1

Goodwrench Plus
2000 Chevrolet Monte Carlo

	Scale	LE	Value		Scale	LE	Value
❏ Action	1:18		$120	❏ Winner's Circle Deluxe			
❏ Action ▲	1:24		$60	(white outlining)	1:64		$6
❏ Action	1:64		$12	❏ Winner's Circle			
❏ Action/RCCA	1:64		$16	Sneak Preview	1:24		$16
❏ Action/RCCA Elite	1:24		$115	❏ Winner's Circle			
❏ Revell Collection	1:24		$50	Sneak Preview	1:64		$5
❏ Revell Collection	1:64		$13	❏ Winner's Circle			
❏ Revell Collection Club	1:24		$30	Speedweeks	1:64		$5
❏ Winner's Circle	1:24		N/E	❏			
❏ Winner's Circle	1:64		$6	❏			
❏ Winner's Circle Deluxe				❏			
(w/hood)	1:64		$10	❏			

How Many: **Total Value:**   **Notes:**

Page Totals: **How Many**   **Total Value**

COLLECTOR'S
VALUE GUIDE™

2

Goodwrench Plus
2000 Chevrolet Monte Carlo

	Scale	LE	Value		Scale	LE	Value
❑ Action/RCCA (platinum) ▲	1:24		N/E	❑			
❑				❑			

How Many: | **Total Value:** | **Notes:**

3

**PHOTO
UNAVAILABLE**

Goodwrench Plus
2000 Chevrolet Monte Carlo

	Scale	LE	Value		Scale	LE	Value
❑ Action (QVC, gold)	1:24		$200	❑			
❑				❑			

How Many: | **Total Value:** | **Notes:**

COLLECTOR'S
VALUE GUIDE™

Page Totals:	How Many	Total Value

4

2000

Goodwrench Plus – Test Car
2000 Chevrolet Monte Carlo

	Scale	LE	Value		Scale	LE	Value
❑ Action/RCCA Elite ▲	1:24		$185	❑			
❑ Revell Collection	1:24		$200	❑			
❑				❑			

How Many: / **Total Value:** $185 **Notes:**

5

Peter Max
2000 Chevrolet Monte Carlo

	Scale	LE	Value		Scale	LE	Value
❑ Action	1:18		$90	❑ Revell Collection	1:43		$35
❑ Action ▲	1:24		$65	❑ Revell Collection	1:64		N/E
❑ Action	1:64		$25	❑			
❑ Action/RCCA	1:64		$38	❑			
❑ Action/RCCA Elite	1:24		$140	❑			
❑ Revell Collection	1:24		$60	❑			

How Many: **Total Value:** **Notes:**

Page Totals: | **How Many** / | **Total Value** $140

COLLECTOR'S
VALUE GUIDE™

2000

Peter Max
2000 Chevrolet Monte Carlo

	Scale	LE	Value			Scale	LE	Value
❑ Action				❑				
(QVC, gold detailing) ▲	1:24		$160	❑				
❑				❑				

How Many: **Total Value:**   **Notes:**

7

Taz No Bull
2000 Chevrolet Monte Carlo

	Scale	LE	Value			Scale	LE	Value
❑ Action	1:18		$90	❑ Revell Collection Club		1:18		$100
❑ Action	1:24		$75	❑ Revell Collection Club		1:24		$80
❑ Action	1:32		$50	❑ Winner's Circle		1:24		$18
❑ Action	1:64		$20	❑ Winner's Circle Deluxe		1:64		$38
❑ Action/RCCA	1:64		$22	❑				
❑ Action/RCCA Elite	1:24		$140	❑				
❑ Revell Collection	1:43		$33	❑				
❑ Revell Collection ▲	1:64		$15	❑				

How Many: **Total Value:**   **Notes:**

2000

8

Taz No Bull
2000 Chevrolet Monte Carlo

	Scale	LE	Value		Scale	LE	Value
❏ Action				❏			
(QVC, chrome) ▲	1:24		$145	❏			
❏				❏			

How Many:	Total Value:	Notes:

9

Taz No Bull
2000 Chevrolet Monte Carlo

	Scale	LE	Value		Scale	LE	Value
❏ Action				❏			
(QVC, gold) ▲	1:24		$220	❏			
❏				❏			

How Many:	Total Value:	Notes:

Page Totals:	How Many	Total Value

COLLECTOR'S
VALUE GUIDE™

Other Collectibles

Dale Earnhardt fans not only collect die-cast cars but seek out other Earnhardt collectibles, too. The choices are plentiful, from die-cast banks to replica cars made out of crystal. Die-hard collectors may even build racing scenes with duallies, pit wagons and transporters, all adding realistic touches to their die-cast car racing collections.

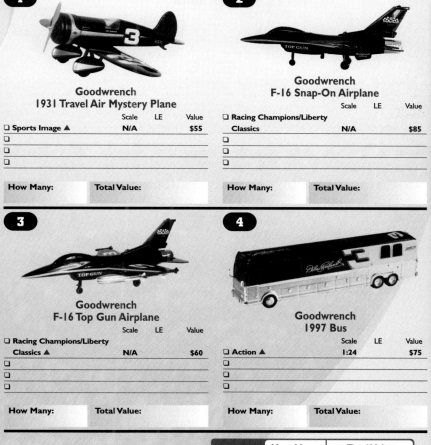

1

Goodwrench
1931 Travel Air Mystery Plane

	Scale	LE	Value
☐ Sports Image ▲	N/A		$55
☐			
☐			
☐			

How Many: Total Value:

2

Goodwrench
F-16 Snap-On Airplane

	Scale	LE	Value
☐ Racing Champions/Liberty Classics	N/A		$85
☐			
☐			
☐			

How Many: Total Value:

3

Goodwrench
F-16 Top Gun Airplane

	Scale	LE	Value
☐ Racing Champions/Liberty Classics ▲	N/A		$60
☐			
☐			
☐			

How Many: Total Value:

4

Goodwrench
1997 Bus

	Scale	LE	Value
☐ Action ▲	1:24		$75
☐			
☐			
☐			

How Many: Total Value:

COLLECTOR'S VALUE GUIDE™

Page Totals:	How Many	Total Value

Banks – Cars

1

1937 Chevrolet Roadster

	Scale	LE	Value
☐ Racing Champions/Liberty Classics ▲	1:25		$95
☐			
☐			
☐			

How Many:	Total Value:

2

1955 Chevrolet Nomad

	Scale	LE	Value
☐ Action ▲	1:24		$75
☐			
☐			
☐			

How Many:	Total Value:

3

Pink Ford
1956 Ford Victoria

	Scale	LE	Value
☐ Action	1:24		$50
☐ Action/RCCA ▲	1:24		$88
☐			
☐			
☐			

How Many:	Total Value:

4

RPM
1975 Dodge

	Scale	LE	Value
☐ Action	1:24		$55
☐ Action/RCCA ▲	1:24		$65
☐			
☐			
☐			

How Many:	Total Value:

5

Army
1976 Chevrolet Malibu

	Scale	LE	Value
☐ Action ▲	1:24		$65
☐ Action/RCCA	1:24		$65
☐			
☐			
☐			

How Many:	Total Value:

6

Hy-Gain
1976 Chevrolet Malibu

	Scale	LE	Value
☐ Action	1:24		$65
☐ Action/RCCA ▲	1:24		$70
☐			
☐			
☐			

How Many:	Total Value:

Page Totals:	How Many	Total Value

COLLECTOR'S
VALUE GUIDE™

1

Wrangler
1981 Pontiac Grand Prix

	Scale	LE	Value
❑ Action/RCCA (#2)	1:24		$205
❑			
❑			
❑			

How Many: Total Value:

2

Wrangler
1981 Pontiac Grand Prix

	Scale	LE	Value
❑ Action/RCCA (#3)	1:24		$200
❑			
❑			
❑			

How Many: Total Value:

3

Wrangler
1982 Ford Thunderbird

	Scale	LE	Value
❑ Action	1:24		$200
❑ Action (blue box) ▲	1:24		$175
❑			
❑			
❑			

How Many: Total Value:

4

Wrangler
1983 Ford Thunderbird

	Scale	LE	Value
❑ Action/RCCA ▲	1:24		$265
❑			
❑			
❑			

How Many: Total Value:

5

Wrangler
1984 Chevrolet Monte Carlo

	Scale	LE	Value
❑ Action	1:24		$250
❑ Action (blue box)	1:24		$250
❑			
❑			
❑			

How Many: Total Value:

6

Wrangler Daytona
1984 Chevrolet Monte Carlo

	Scale	LE	Value
❑ Action ▲	1:24		$135
❑			
❑			
❑			

How Many: Total Value:

COLLECTOR'S VALUE GUIDE™

Page Totals:	How Many	Total Value

Banks – Cars

1

Wrangler
1985 Chevrolet Monte Carlo

	Scale	LE	Value
❏ Action/RCCA ▲	1:24		$260
❏			
❏			
❏			

How Many: ___   Total Value: ___

2

PHOTO
UNAVAILABLE

Wrangler
1987 Chevrolet Monte Carlo Fastback

	Scale	LE	Value
❏ Action/RCCA	1:24		$315
❏			
❏			
❏			

How Many: ___   Total Value: ___

3

Goodwrench
1988 Chevrolet Monte Carlo Fastback

	Scale	LE	Value
❏ Action ▲	1:24		$600
❏			
❏			
❏			

How Many: ___   Total Value: ___

4

Lowe's Foods
1989 Pontiac Grand Prix

	Scale	LE	Value
❏ Action/RCCA ▲	1:24		$200
❏			
❏			
❏			

How Many: ___   Total Value: ___

5

Goodwrench
1991 Chevrolet Lumina

	Scale	LE	Value
❏ Racing Champions ▲	1:24		N/E
❏			
❏			
❏			

How Many: ___   Total Value: ___

6

Goodwrench
1993 Chevrolet Lumina

	Scale	LE	Value
❏ Racing Champions ▲	1:24		N/E
❏			
❏			
❏			

How Many: ___   Total Value: ___

Page Totals:	How Many	Total Value

COLLECTOR'S
VALUE GUIDE™

1

PHOTO UNAVAILABLE

Goodwrench
1994 Chevrolet Lumina

	Scale	LE	Value
❏ Racing Champions	1:24		$220
❏ Racing Champion (6-time)	1:24		$205
❏			
❏			

How Many: Total Value:

2

Goodwrench – Busch Series
1994 Chevrolet Lumina

	Scale	LE	Value
❏ Action	1:24		N/E
❏ Action/RCCA	1:24		$180
❏ Action/Sports Image ▲	1:24		$285
❏ Racing Champions	1:24		$190
❏			

How Many: Total Value:

3

Goodwrench
1995 Chevrolet Monte Carlo

	Scale	LE	Value
❏ Action	1:24		$165
❏ Action			
(w/out headlight rings) ▲	1:24		$210
❏			
❏			

How Many: Total Value:

4

Winston Silver Select
1995 Chevrolet Monte Carlo

	Scale	LE	Value
❏ Action (black wheels)	1:24		$475
❏ Action (GM Parts on hood) ▲	1:24		N/E
❏ Action (red wheels)	1:24		$475
❏			
❏			

How Many: Total Value:

5

ACDelco
1996 Chevrolet Monte Carlo

	Scale	LE	Value
❏ Action/RCCA ▲	1:24		$100
❏			
❏			
❏			
❏			

How Many: Total Value:

6

Goodwrench
1996 Chevrolet Monte Carlo

	Scale	LE	Value
❏ Action/RCCA ▲	1:24		$85
❏			
❏			
❏			

How Many: Total Value:

Page Totals:	How Many	Total Value

Banks – Cars

Collector's Value Guide™ – Dale Earnhardt®

1

Olympics
1996 Chevrolet Monte Carlo

	Scale	LE	Value
❏ Action	1:24		N/E
❏ Action (w/out base) ▲	1:24		$125
❏			
❏			
❏			

How Many: _____ Total Value: _____

2

ACDelco
1997 Chevrolet Monte Carlo

	Scale	LE	Value
❏ Action	1:24		$90
❏ Action/RCCA ▲	1:24		N/E
❏			
❏			
❏			

How Many: _____ Total Value: _____

3

Goodwrench
1997 Chevrolet Monte Carlo

	Scale	LE	Value
❏ Action ▲	1:24		$75
❏			
❏			
❏			

How Many: _____ Total Value: _____

4

Goodwrench Plus
1997 Chevrolet Monte Carlo

	Scale	LE	Value
❏ Action	1:24		$75
❏ Action/RCCA ▲	1:24		N/E
❏			
❏			
❏			

How Many: _____ Total Value: _____

5

Wheaties
1997 Chevrolet Monte Carlo

	Scale	LE	Value
❏ Action ▲	1:24		$120
❏			
❏			
❏			

How Many: _____ Total Value: _____

6

Bass Pro Shops
1998 Chevrolet Monte Carlo

	Scale	LE	Value
❏ Action	1:24		$115
❏ Action/RCCA ▲	1:24		$125
❏			
❏			
❏			

How Many: _____ Total Value: _____

Page Totals: How Many _____ Total Value _____

COLLECTOR'S VALUE GUIDE™

1

Coca-Cola
1998 Chevrolet Monte Carlo

	Scale	LE	Value
❏ Action	1:24		$70
❏ Action/RCCA ▲	1:24		$90
❏			
❏			
❏			

How Many: Total Value:

2

Goodwrench Plus
1998 Chevrolet Monte Carlo

	Scale	LE	Value
❏ Action ▲	1:24		$50
❏ Action/RCCA	1:24		$80
❏			
❏			
❏			

How Many: Total Value:

3

Goodwrench Plus – Daytona 500
1998 Chevrolet Monte Carlo

	Scale	LE	Value
❏ Action ▲	1:24		$70
❏ Action/RCCA	1:24		$82
❏			
❏			
❏			

How Many: Total Value:

4

Goodwrench Plus
1999 Chevrolet Monte Carlo

	Scale	LE	Value
❏ Action ▲	1:24		$60
❏ Action/RCCA	1:24		$95
❏			
❏			
❏			

How Many: Total Value:

5

Goodwrench Plus – 25th Anniversary
1999 Chevrolet Monte Carlo

	Scale	LE	Value
❏ Action	1:24		$60
❏ Action/RCCA ▲	1:24		$95
❏			
❏			
❏			

How Many: Total Value:

6

Goodwrench Plus – Last Lap
1999 Chevrolet Monte Carlo

	Scale	LE	Value
❏ Action ▲	1:24		$95
❏ Action/RCCA	1:24		$145
❏			
❏			
❏			

How Many: Total Value:

COLLECTOR'S
VALUE GUIDE™

Page Totals:	How Many	Total Value

Collector's Value Guide™ – Dale Earnhardt®

Banks – Cars/Car Sets

1

Goodwrench Plus – Sign Car
1999 Chevrolet Monte Carlo

	Scale	LE	Value
❑ Action	1:24		$60
❑ Action/RCCA ▲	1:24		$95
❑			
❑			
❑			

How Many: ____ Total Value: ____

2

Wrangler Colors
1999 Chevrolet Monte Carlo

	Scale	LE	Value
❑ Action	1:24		$70
❑ Action/RCCA ▲	1:24		$150
❑			
❑			
❑			

How Many: ____ Total Value: ____

3

Goodwrench Plus
2000 Chevrolet Monte Carlo

	Scale	LE	Value
❑ Action ▲	1:24		$70
❑ Action/RCCA	1:24		$75
❑			
❑			
❑			

How Many: ____ Total Value: ____

4

Peter Max
2000 Chevrolet Monte Carlo

	Scale	LE	Value
❑ Action/RCCA ▲	1:24		$75
❑			
❑			
❑			

How Many: ____ Total Value: ____

5

Taz No Bull
2000 Chevrolet Monte Carlo

	Scale	LE	Value
❑ Action	1:24		$75
❑ Action/RCCA ▲	1:24		$85
❑			
❑			
❑			

How Many: ____ Total Value: ____

6

Winston Silver Select
1995 Chevrolet Monte Carlo

	Scale	LE	Value
❑ Action (desk set) ▲	1:24		N/E
❑			
❑			
❑			

How Many: ____ Total Value: ____

Page Totals:	How Many	Total Value

COLLECTOR'S
VALUE GUIDE™

1

Coca-Cola
1998 Chevrolet Monte Carlo

	Scale	LE	Value
❑ Revell Collection			
(w/1:64 car) ▲	1:24		N/E
❑			
❑			
❑			

How Many: Total Value:

2

Taz No Bull
2000 Chevrolet Monte Carlo

	Scale	LE	Value
❑ Revell Collection			
(w/1:64 car) ▲	1:24		N/E
❑			
❑			
❑			

How Many: Total Value:

3

Goodwrench
1996 Dually

	Scale	LE	Value
❑ Action/RCCA ▲	1:24		$75
❑ Brookfield			
Collector's Guild	1:25		$75
❑			
❑			

How Many: Total Value:

4

PHOTO
UNAVAILABLE

Olympics
1996 Dually

	Scale	LE	Value
❑ Brookfield			
Collector's Guild	1:25		$75
❑			
❑			
❑			

How Many: Total Value:

5

PHOTO
UNAVAILABLE

Racing Thunder
1996 Dually

	Scale	LE	Value
❑ Brookfield			
Collector's Guild	1:24		$85
❑			
❑			
❑			

How Many: Total Value:

6

Wheaties
1997 Dually

	Scale	LE	Value
❑ Action/RCCA ▲	1:24		$105
❑			
❑			
❑			

How Many: Total Value:

1

Goodwrench Racing Dually

	Scale	LE	Value
❑ Action/RCCA ▲	1:24		N/E
❑			
❑			
❑			

How Many: Total Value:

2

7 & 7 Earnhardt/Petty 1995 Gas Pump

	Scale	LE	Value
❑ Action ▲	1:16		$60
❑			
❑			
❑			

How Many: Total Value:

3

Olympics 1996 Gas Pump

	Scale	LE	Value
❑ Action ▲	1:16		$45
❑			
❑			
❑			

How Many: Total Value:

4

Wheaties 1997 Gas Pump

	Scale	LE	Value
❑ Action ▲	1:16		$60
❑			
❑			
❑			

How Many: Total Value:

5

Bass Pro Shops 1998 Gas Pump

	Scale	LE	Value
❑ Action ▲	1:16		$52
❑			
❑			
❑			

How Many: Total Value:

6

Coca-Cola 1998 Gas Pump

	Scale	LE	Value
❑ Action ▲	1:16		$50
❑			
❑			
❑			

How Many: Total Value:

Page Totals: How Many   Total Value

COLLECTOR'S VALUE GUIDE™

1

Goodwrench Plus
1998 Gas Pump

	Scale	LE	Value
☐ Action ▲	1:16		$48
☐			
☐			
☐			

How Many: ___ Total Value: ___

2

Goodwrench Plus – 25th Anniversary
1999 Gas Pump

	Scale	LE	Value
☐ Action ▲	1:16		$45
☐			
☐			
☐			

How Many: ___ Total Value: ___

3

Wrangler Colors
1999 Gas Pump

	Scale	LE	Value
☐ Action ▲	1:16		$50
☐			
☐			
☐			

How Many: ___ Total Value: ___

4

Peter Max
2000 Gas Pump

	Scale	LE	Value
☐ Action ▲	1:16		$50
☐			
☐			
☐			

How Many: ___ Total Value: ___

5

Taz No Bull
2000 Gas Pump

	Scale	LE	Value
☐ Action ▲	1:16		$60
☐			
☐			
☐			

How Many: ___ Total Value: ___

6

Goodwrench
Golf Cart

	Scale	LE	Value
☐ Georgia Marketing Promotions ▲	1:24		$60
☐			
☐			
☐			

How Many: ___ Total Value: ___

Banks – Pit Wagons

1

PHOTO UNAVAILABLE

**Goodwrench
1994 Pit Wagon**

	Scale	LE	Value
☐ Action/RCCA	1:16		N/E
☐			
☐			
☐			

How Many: Total Value:

2

PHOTO UNAVAILABLE

**7 & 7 Earnhardt/Petty
1995 Pit Wagon**

	Scale	LE	Value
☐ Action	1:16		$75
☐			
☐			
☐			

How Many: Total Value:

3

**Goodwrench
1995 Pit Wagon**

	Scale	LE	Value
☐ Action ▲	1:16		$60
☐			
☐			
☐			

How Many: Total Value:

4

**Goodwrench – Quick Lube
1995 Pit Wagon**

	Scale	LE	Value
☐ Action/RCCA ▲	1:16		$55
☐			
☐			
☐			

How Many: Total Value:

5

**Goodwrench
1996 Pit Wagon**

	Scale	LE	Value
☐ Action ▲	1:16		$75
☐			
☐			
☐			

How Many: Total Value:

6

**Wheaties
1997 Pit Wagon**

	Scale	LE	Value
☐ Action ▲	1:16		$85
☐			
☐			
☐			

How Many: Total Value:

Page Totals:	How Many	Total Value

COLLECTOR'S
VALUE GUIDE™

Collector's Value Guide™ – Dale Earnhardt®

1

Bass Pro Shops
1998 Pit Wagon

	Scale	LE	Value
❏ Action ▲	1:16		$80
❏			
❏			
❏			

How Many: **Total Value:**

2

Goodwrench Plus
1999 Pit Wagon

	Scale	LE	Value
❏ Action ▲	1:16		$55
❏			
❏			
❏			

How Many: **Total Value:**

3

Wrangler Colors
1999 Pit Wagon

	Scale	LE	Value
❏ Action ▲	1:16		$45
❏			
❏			
❏			

How Many: **Total Value:**

4

Peter Max
2000 Pit Wagon

	Scale	LE	Value
❏ Action ▲	1:16		$50
❏			
❏			
❏			

How Many: **Total Value:**

5

Taz No Bull
2000 Pit Wagon

	Scale	LE	Value
❏ Action ▲	1:16		$68
❏			
❏			
❏			

How Many: **Total Value:**

6

7 & 7 Earnhardt/Petty
1995 Chevrolet Suburban

	Scale	LE	Value
❏ Brookfield			
Collector's Guild ▲	1:25		N/E
❏			
❏			
❏			

How Many: **Total Value:**

COLLECTOR'S
VALUE GUIDE™

Page Totals:	How Many	Total Value

Banks – Pit Wagons/Suburbans

1

Goodwrench
1995 Chevrolet Suburban

	Scale	LE	Value
❑ Brookfield			
Collector's Guild (7-time) ▲	1:25		$80
❑			
❑			
❑			

How Many: ___ Total Value: ___

2

Goodwrench
1995 Chevrolet Suburban

	Scale	LE	Value
❑ Brookfield			
Collector's Guild (white) ▲	1:25		$475
❑			
❑			
❑			

How Many: ___ Total Value: ___

3

Winston Silver Select
1995 Chevrolet Suburban

	Scale	LE	Value
❑ Brookfield			
Collector's Guild ▲	1:25		$275
❑			
❑			
❑			

How Many: ___ Total Value: ___

4

Bass Pro Shops
1998 Chevrolet Tahoe

	Scale	LE	Value
❑ Brookfield			
Collector's Guild ▲	1:25		$50
❑			
❑			
❑			

How Many: ___ Total Value: ___

5

Goodwrench
1993 Transporter

	Scale	LE	Value
❑ Racing Champions/			
Kenworth ▲	1:64		N/E
❑			
❑			
❑			

How Many: ___ Total Value: ___

6

Goodwrench
1997 Chevrolet Monte Carlo
Ceramic Car

	Scale	LE	Value
❑ Action/RCCA			
("crash car") ▲	1:12		$200
❑			
❑			
❑			

How Many: ___ Total Value: ___

Page Totals:	How Many	Total Value

1

Taz No Bull
2000 Chevrolet Monte Carlo
Ceramic Car

	Scale	LE	Value
❏ Action ▲	1:12		$165
❏ Action	1:24		$150
❏			
❏			
❏			

How Many: **Total Value:**

2

Goodwrench Plus
1957 Chevrolet Bel Air
Commemorative Car

	Scale	LE	Value
❏ Winner's Circle			
(convertible) ▲	1:64		$5
❏			
❏			
❏			

How Many: **Total Value:**

3

Goodwrench Plus
1957 Chevrolet Bel Air
Commemorative Car

	Scale	LE	Value
❏ Winner's Circle (hard top) ▲	1:64		$7
❏			
❏			
❏			

How Many: **Total Value:**

4

Goodwrench Plus
1957 Chevrolet Bel Air
Commemorative Car

	Scale	LE	Value
❏ Winner's Circle Cool			
Customs Series (silver) ▲	1:64		$5
❏			
❏			
❏			

How Many: **Total Value:**

5

Goodwrench/DuPont
1995 Chevrolet Monte Carlos
Commemorative Cars

	Scale	LE	Value
❏ Action ▲	1:64		$42
❏			
❏			
❏			

How Many: **Total Value:**

6

Goodwrench – "Team Up To Win"
1997 Chevrolet Monte Carlo
Commemorative Car

	Scale	LE	Value
❏ Action ▲	1:24		N/E
❏			
❏			
❏			

How Many: **Total Value:**

Collector's Value Guide™ – Dale Earnhardt®

Commemorative Cars/Crystal Cars *(vertical sidebar text)*

1

Goodwrench Plus – 25th Anniversary
1999 Chevrolet Corvette
Commemorative Car

	Scale	LE	Value
❏ Brookfield			
Collector's Guild ▲	1:24		N/E
❏			
❏			
❏			

How Many: Total Value:

2

Winston Cup Series
1994 Transporter
Commemorative Transporter

	Scale	LE	Value
❏ Action ▲	1:64		$105
❏			
❏			
❏			

How Many: Total Value:

3

Bass Pro Shops
1998 Chevrolet Monte Carlo
Crystal Car

	Scale	LE	Value
❏ Action ▲	1:24		$60
❏			
❏			
❏			

How Many: Total Value:

4

Coca-Cola
1998 Chevrolet Monte Carlo
Crystal Car

	Scale	LE	Value
❏ Action ▲	1:24		$60
❏			
❏			
❏			

How Many: Total Value:

5

Goodwrench Plus
1999 Chevrolet Monte Carlo
Crystal Car

	Scale	LE	Value
❏ Action ▲	1:24		$65
❏			
❏			
❏			

How Many: Total Value:

6

PHOTO UNAVAILABLE

Goodwrench Plus – 25th Anniversary
1999 Chevrolet Monte Carlo
Crystal Car

	Scale	LE	Value
❏ Action	1:24		$60
❏			
❏			
❏			

How Many: Total Value:

Page Totals:	How Many	Total Value

COLLECTOR'S **VALUE GUIDE**™

1

Wrangler Colors
1999 Chevrolet Monte Carlo
Crystal Car

	Scale	LE	Value
☐ Action ▲	1:24		$65
☐			
☐			
☐			

How Many: _____ Total Value: _____

2

Taz No Bull
2000 Chevrolet Monte Carlo
Crystal Car

	Scale	LE	Value
☐ Action ▲	1:24		$75
☐			
☐			
☐			

How Many: _____ Total Value: _____

3

Goodwrench
1994 Dually w/Trailer

	Scale	LE	Value
☐ Action	1:64		$35
☐ Action/RCI ▲	1:64		$35
☐ Action/Sports Image	1:64		$35
☐			
☐			

How Many: _____ Total Value: _____

4

Goodwrench
1995 Dually

	Scale	LE	Value
☐ Action ▲	1:24		$45
☐			
☐			

How Many: _____ Total Value: _____

5

Goodwrench
1995 Dually w/Trailer

	Scale	LE	Value
☐ Action (7-time) ▲	1:64		$25
☐			
☐			
☐			

How Many: _____ Total Value: _____

6

Goodwrench – Brickyard 400
1995 Dually

	Scale	LE	Value
☐ Brookfield			
Collector's Guild ▲	1:24		N/E
☐			
☐			
☐			

How Many: _____ Total Value: _____

Duallies

1

Winston Silver Select
1995 Dually

	Scale	LE	Value
❑ Brookfield			
Collector's Guild	1:25		$35
❑ Brookfield			
Collector's Guild			
(w/trailer & car)	1:25		$50
❑			

How Many: **Total Value:**

2

Goodwrench
1996 Dually

	Scale	LE	Value
❑ Action	1:64		$35
❑ Action/RCCA (w/trailer)	1:64		$40
❑			
❑			
❑			

How Many: **Total Value:**

3

Wheaties
1997 Dually

	Scale	LE	Value
❑ Action ▲	1:64		$45
❑			
❑			
❑			

How Many: **Total Value:**

4

Wheaties
1997 Dually w/Trailer

	Scale	LE	Value
❑ Action ▲	1:64		$75
❑			
❑			
❑			

How Many: **Total Value:**

5

Bass Pro Shops
1998 Dually w/Trailer

	Scale	LE	Value
❑ Action (open trailer) ▲	1:64		$50
❑			
❑			
❑			

How Many: **Total Value:**

6

Bass Pro Shops
1998 Dually w/Trailer

	Scale	LE	Value
❑ Action (enclosed trailer) ▲	1:64		N/E
❑			
❑			
❑			

How Many: **Total Value:**

Page Totals:	How Many	Total Value

COLLECTOR'S
VALUE GUIDE™

1

Goodwrench Plus
1999 Dually w/Trailer & Car

	Scale	LE	Value
❏ Action ▲	1:64		$55
❏			
❏			
❏			

How Many: Total Value:

2

Goodwrench Plus – 25th Anniversary
1999 Dually w/Trailer & Car

	Scale	LE	Value
❏ Brookfield			
Collector's Guild ▲	1:24		N/E
❏			
❏			

How Many: Total Value:

3

Wrangler Colors
1999 Dually w/Trailer

	Scale	LE	Value
❏ Action ▲	1:64		$30
❏			
❏			
❏			

How Many: Total Value:

4

Taz No Bull
2000 Dually w/Trailer & Car

	Scale	LE	Value
❏ Action	1:64		$40
❏ Brookfield			
Collector's Guild ▲	1:24		N/E
❏			
❏			

How Many: Total Value:

5

Taz No Bull
2000 Dually w/Trailer & Car

	Scale	LE	Value
❏ Brookfield			
Collector's Guild (silver) ▲	1:24		N/E
❏			
❏			
❏			

How Many: Total Value:

6

Goodwrench
Dually w/Trailer

	Scale	LE	Value
❏ Action	1:64		$65
❏ Action/Sports Image ▲	1:64		$65
❏			
❏			
❏			

How Many: Total Value:

Page Totals:	How Many	Total Value

Duallies/Pedal Cars/Pit Scenes

1

Goodwrench Racing Dually w/Trailer

	Scale	LE	Value
❑ Action ▲	1:64		$125
❑			
❑			
❑			

How Many: ___ **Total Value:** ___

2

Wrangler Colors 1999 Pedal Car

	Scale	LE	Value
❑ Action ▲	1:43		N/E
❑ Action/RCCA (w/trailer)	1:43		N/E
❑			
❑			

How Many: ___ **Total Value:** ___

3

Taz No Bull 2000 Pedal Car

	Scale	LE	Value
❑ Action ▲	1:43		N/E
❑ Action/RCCA (w/trailer)	1:43		N/E
❑			
❑			
❑			

How Many: ___ **Total Value:** ___

4

PHOTO UNAVAILABLE

Wrangler – "Moving Into Position" 1987 Pit Scene

	Scale	LE	Value
❑ Winner's Circle Pit Row			
25th Anniversary	1:64		$12
❑			
❑			
❑			

How Many: ___ **Total Value:** ___

5

PHOTO UNAVAILABLE

Goodwrench – "Tires Off" 1993 Pit Scene

	Scale	LE	Value
❑ Winner's Circle Pit Row			
25th Anniversary	1:64		$12
❑			
❑			
❑			

How Many: ___ **Total Value:** ___

6

PHOTO UNAVAILABLE

Goodwrench – "Four Tire Stop" 1995 Pit Scene

	Scale	LE	Value
❑ Winner's Circle Pit Row			
25th Anniversary (Atlanta)	1:64		$12
❑ Winner's Circle Pit Row			
25th Anniversary (Brickyard)	1:64		$12
❑			

How Many: ___ **Total Value:** ___

Page Totals:	How Many	Total Value

COLLECTOR'S VALUE GUIDE™

1

Bass Pro Shops – "Two Tire Stop"
1998 Pit Scene

	Scale	LE	Value
☐ Winner's Circle Pit Row ▲	1:64		$12
☐			
☐			
☐			

How Many: ___   Total Value: ___

2

Coca-Cola – "Tires Off"
1998 Pit Scene

	Scale	LE	Value
☐ Winner's Circle Pit Row ▲	1:64		$12
☐			
☐			
☐			

How Many: ___   Total Value: ___

3

Goodwrench Plus –
"Custom Infield Donuts"
1998 Pit Scene

	Scale	LE	Value
☐ Winner's Circle Pit Row ▲	1:64		$12
☐			
☐			
☐			

How Many: ___   Total Value: ___

4

Goodwrench Plus – "Moving Into Position"
1998 Pit Scene

	Scale	LE	Value
☐ Winner's Circle Pit Row ▲	1:64		$12
☐			
☐			
☐			

How Many: ___   Total Value: ___

5

Goodwrench Plus – "Dale Earnhardt"
1999 Pit Scene

	Scale	LE	Value
☐ Winner's Circle Pit Row 25th Anniversary ▲	1:64		$9
☐			
☐			
☐			

How Many: ___   Total Value: ___

6

Goodwrench Plus – "Pulling In"
1999 Pit Scene

	Scale	LE	Value
☐ Winner's Circle Pit Row ▲	1:64		$12
☐			
☐			
☐			

How Many: ___   Total Value: ___

Page Totals:	How Many	Total Value

Pit Scenes/Roaring Racers

1

PHOTO UNAVAILABLE

Goodwrench Plus – "Two-Tire Stop/Start Of Season" 1999 Pit Scene

	Scale	LE	Value
❏ Winner's Circle Pit Row	1:64		$12
❏			
❏			
❏			

How Many: ___ Total Value: ___

2

Wrangler Colors – "Four Tire Stop" 1999 Pit Scene

	Scale	LE	Value
❏ Winner's Circle Pit Row ▲	1:64		$12
❏			
❏			
❏			

How Many: ___ Total Value: ___

3

Goodwrench – "Garage Scene" 2000 Pit Scene

	Scale	LE	Value
❏ Winners Circle ▲	1:43		$9
❏			
❏			
❏			

How Many: ___ Total Value: ___

4

Goodwrench Pit Scene

	Scale	LE	Value
❏ Racing Champions ▲	1:64		$12
❏			
❏			
❏			

How Many: ___ Total Value: ___

5

PHOTO UNAVAILABLE

Goodwrench 1990 Roaring Racer

	Scale	LE	Value
❏ Racing Champions	1:64		$100
❏			
❏			
❏			

How Many: ___ Total Value: ___

Page Totals:	How Many	Total Value

1

PHOTO UNAVAILABLE

**7 & 7 Earnhardt/Petty
1979 Car Set**

	Scale	LE	Value
☐ Action	1:64		$15
☐			
☐			
☐			

How Many: **Total Value:**

2

PHOTO UNAVAILABLE

**7 & 7 Earnhardt/Petty
1995 Car Set**

	Scale	LE	Value
☐ Action	1:64		N/E
☐			
☐			
☐			

How Many: **Total Value:**

3

PHOTO UNAVAILABLE

1996 Collector's Set

Rod Osterlund 1978 Chevrolet Monte Carlo – Mike Curb 1980 Oldsmobile 442 – Mike Curb 1980 Chevrolet Monte Carlo – Wrangler 1981 Pontiac – Wrangler 1982 Ford Thunderbird – Wrangler 1983 Ford Thunderbird – Wrangler 1984 Chevrolet Monte Carlo – Wrangler 1986 Chevrolet Monte Carlo – Goodwrench 1988 Chevrolet Camaro – Goodwrench 1988 Chevrolet Monte Carlo – Goodwrench Busch Series 1988 Chevrolet Monte Carlo – Lowe's Foods 1989 Pontiac Grand Prix – Goodwrench 1990 Chevrolet Lumina – Winston Silver Select 1995 Chevrolet Monte Carlo – Goodwrench 1996 Chevrolet Monte Carlo – Olympic 1996 Chevrolet Monte Carlo

	Scale	LE	Value			Scale	LE	Value
☐ Action ▲	1:64		$305	☐				

How Many: **Total Value:** **Notes:**

Page Totals:	How Many	Total Value

Sets – Cars

1

Olympics
1996 Car Set

	Scale	LE	Value
❏ Brookfield			
Collector's Guild ▲	1:25		$165
❏			
❏			
❏			

How Many: ___ Total Value: ___

2

Goodwrench
1999 Boat, Car & Plane Set

	Scale	LE	Value
❏ Winner's Circle			
Fantasy Pack ▲	1:64		N/E
❏			
❏			
❏			

How Many: ___ Total Value: ___

3

Wrangler Colors
1999 Boat, Car & Plane Set

	Scale	LE	Value
❏ Winner's Circle			
Fantasy Pack ▲	1:64		$10
❏			
❏			
❏			

How Many: ___ Total Value: ___

4

Wrangler Colors/Goodwrench Plus
1999 Car Set

	Scale	LE	Value
❏ Brookfield			
Collector's Guild	1:25		N/E
❏ Winner's Circle ▲	1:64		$10
❏			
❏			

How Many: ___ Total Value: ___

5

Goodwrench – Pole Winner Pair
Earnhardt/Gordon Car Set

	Scale	LE	Value
❏ Action ▲	1:64		$44
❏			
❏			
❏			

How Many: ___ Total Value: ___

Page Totals:	How Many	Total Value

Collector's Value Guide™ – Dale Earnhardt®

1

Mike Curb
1980 Car & Figurine Set
	Scale	LE	Value
❑ Winner's Circle			
Championship Legacy	1:64		$12
❑			
❑			
❑			

How Many: ___ Total Value: ___

2

Wrangler
1986 Car & Figurine Set
	Scale	LE	Value
❑ Winner's Circle			
Championship Legacy ▲	1:64		$14
❑			
❑			
❑			

How Many: ___ Total Value: ___

3

Wrangler
1987 Car & Figurine Set
	Scale	LE	Value
❑ Winner's Circle			
Championship Legacy ▲	1:64		$7
❑			
❑			
❑			

How Many: ___ Total Value: ___

4

Goodwrench
1990 Car & Figurine Set
	Scale	LE	Value
❑ Winner's Circle			
Championship Legacy	1:64		$7
❑			
❑			
❑			

How Many: ___ Total Value: ___

5

Goodwrench
1991 Car & Figurine Set
	Scale	LE	Value
❑ Winner's Circle			
Championship Legacy	1:64		$7
❑			
❑			
❑			

How Many: ___ Total Value: ___

6

Goodwrench
1993 Car & Figurine Set
	Scale	LE	Value
❑ Winner's Circle			
Championship Legacy	1:64		$7
❑			
❑			
❑			

How Many: ___ Total Value: ___

COLLECTOR'S VALUE GUIDE™

Page Totals:	How Many	Total Value

Sets – Cars & Figurines/Cars & Tools

1

Goodwrench
1994 Car & Figurine Set

	Scale	LE	Value
❏ Winner's Circle			
Championship Legacy ▲	1:64		$14
❏			
❏			
❏			

How Many: ___ Total Value: ___

2

PHOTO UNAVAILABLE

Goodwrench
1995 Car & Figurine Set

	Scale	LE	Value
❏ Winner's Circle			
Victory Celebration	1:43		$7
❏			
❏			
❏			

How Many: ___ Total Value: ___

3

Coca-Cola
1998 Car & Figurine Set

	Scale	LE	Value
❏ Winner's Circle ▲	1:24		N/E
❏ Winner's Circle			
Championship Legacy	1:24		$7
❏			

How Many: ___ Total Value: ___

4

Goodwrench Plus – Daytona 500
1998 Car & Figurine Set

	Scale	LE	Value
❏ Winner's Circle			
Championship Legacy ▲	1:24		$7
❏			
❏			
❏			

How Many: ___ Total Value: ___

5

Goodwrench Plus – Daytona 500
1998 Car & Figurine Set

	Scale	LE	Value
❏ Winner's Circle			
Victory Celebration ▲	1:43		N/E
❏			
❏			
❏			

How Many: ___ Total Value: ___

6

ACDelco
1996 Car & Tool Set

	Scale	LE	Value
❏ Action/Snap On ▲	1:24		$60
❏			
❏			
❏			

How Many: ___ Total Value: ___

Page Totals:	How Many	Total Value

COLLECTOR'S
VALUE GUIDE™

Collector's Value Guide™ – Dale Earnhardt®

1

Goodwrench Plus
1996 Car & Tool Set

	Scale	LE	Value
❏ Action/Snap On ▲	1:24		$60
❏			
❏			
❏			

How Many: _____ Total Value: _____

2

Olympics
1996 Car & Tool Set

	Scale	LE	Value
❏ Action/Snap On	1:24		N/E
❏			
❏			
❏			

How Many: _____ Total Value: _____

3

Wheaties
1997 Car & Tool Set

	Scale	LE	Value
❏ Action/Snap On	1:24		$165
❏			
❏			
❏			

How Many: _____ Total Value: _____

4

Bass Pro Shops
1998 Car & Tool Set

	Scale	LE	Value
❏ Action/Snap On	1:24		$125
❏			
❏			
❏			

How Many: _____ Total Value: _____

5

Mom 'n' Pops
Dually Set

	Scale	LE	Value
❏ Action	1:64		$135
❏			
❏			
❏			

How Many: _____ Total Value: _____

6

Coca-Cola
1998 Transporter Set

	Scale	LE	Value
❏ Brookfield			
Collector's Guild ▲	1:25		$100
❏			
❏			
❏			

How Many: _____ Total Value: _____

COLLECTOR'S VALUE GUIDE™

Page Totals:	How Many	Total Value

Sets – Cars & Tools/Duallies/Transporters

Collector's Value Guide™ – Dale Earnhardt®

Sets – Trains

1

Olympics
1996 Train Set

	Scale	LE	Value
☐ Revell ▲	N/E		$75
☐			
☐			
☐			

How Many: _____ Total Value: _____

2

Wheaties
1997 Train Set

	Scale	LE	Value
☐ Revell ▲	N/E		$85
☐			
☐			
☐			

How Many: _____ Total Value: _____

3

Bass Pro Shops
1998 Train Set

	Scale	LE	Value
☐ Revell Collection ▲	1:64		$85
☐			
☐			
☐			

How Many: _____ Total Value: _____

4

Coca-Cola
1998 Train Set w/Dale Jr.

	Scale	LE	Value
☐ Revell Collection ▲	1:64		$90
☐			
☐			
☐			

How Many: _____ Total Value: _____

5

Wrangler
Train Set

	Scale	LE	Value
☐ Revell ▲	N/E		$140
☐			
☐			
☐			

How Many: _____ Total Value: _____

Page Totals:	How Many	Total Value

COLLECTOR'S
***VALUE GUIDE*™**

120

1

Goodwrench
1995 Chevrolet Suburban

	Scale	LE	Value
❏ Brookfield			
Collector's Guild ▲	1:25		$40
❏			
❏			
❏			

How Many: **Total Value:**

2

Coca-Cola
1998 Chevrolet Suburban w/Trailer & Car

	Scale	LE	Value
❏ Brookfield			
Collector's Guild ▲	1:25		$100
❏			
❏			
❏			

How Many: **Total Value:**

3

Goodwrench Plus – 25th Anniversary
1999 Chevrolet Suburban w/Trailer & Car

	Scale	LE	Value
❏ Brookfield			
Collector's Guild ▲	1:24		$80
❏			
❏			
❏			

How Many: **Total Value:**

4

Goodwrench
1995 Chevrolet Tahoe

	Scale	LE	Value
❏ Brookfield			
Collector's Guild ▲	1:25		N/E
❏			
❏			
❏			

How Many: **Total Value:**

5

PHOTO
UNAVAILABLE

Winston Silver Select
1995 Chevrolet Tahoe

	Scale	LE	Value
❏ Brookfield			
Collector's Guild	1:25		N/E
❏			
❏			
❏			

How Many: **Total Value:**

COLLECTOR'S
VALUE GUIDE™

Page Totals:	How Many	Total Value

Transporters

1

Wrangler
1985 Transporter

	Scale	LE	Value
☐ Action/Kenworth	1:64		$85
☐ Action/Kenworth ▲	1:96		N/E
☐			
☐			
☐			

How Many: **Total Value:**

2

PHOTO
UNAVAILABLE

Goodwrench Racing
1987 Transporter

	Scale	LE	Value
☐ Nylint Steel	1:25		$260
☐			
☐			

How Many: **Total Value:**

3

Wrangler
1987 Transporter

	Scale	LE	Value
☐ Action/Kenworth	1:64		$85
☐ Action/Kenworth ▲	1:96		N/E
☐			
☐			
☐			

How Many: **Total Value:**

4

PHOTO
UNAVAILABLE

Goodwrench
1989 Transporter

	Scale	LE	Value
☐ Matchbox/White Rose Super Stars	1:87		$250
☐			
☐			
☐			

How Many: **Total Value:**

5

Goodwrench Racing
1990 Transporter

	Scale	LE	Value
☐ Matchbox/White Rose Super Stars	1:87		$100
☐			
☐			
☐			

How Many: **Total Value:**

6

Goodwrench
1991 Transporter

	Scale	LE	Value
☐ Matchbox/White Rose Super Stars (Western Steer) ▲	1:64		N/E
☐ Matchbox/White Rose Super Stars	1:87		$50
☐ Matchbox/White Rose Super Stars (Western Steer)	1:87		$40
☐			

How Many: **Total Value:**

Page Totals:	How Many	Total Value

COLLECTOR'S
VALUE GUIDE™

1

Goodwrench
1992 Transporter

	Scale	LE	Value
❏ Matchbox/White Rose			
Super Stars	1:87		$25
❏ Racing Champions	1:64		$95
❏ Winross (w/cars) ▲	1:64		$200
❏ Winross (w/wooden box)	1:64		$275
❏			

How Many: **Total Value:**

2

Goodwrench
1993 Transporter

	Scale	LE	Value
❏ Ertl ▲	1:64		$45
❏ Racing Champions	1:43		$130
❏ Racing Champions	1:64		$55
❏ Racing Champions	1:64		N/E
(9th Annual Winston)			
❏ Racing Champions (promo)	1:64		$55
❏			

How Many: **Total Value:**

3

Goodwrench
1994 Transporter

	Scale	LE	Value
❏ Matchbox/White Rose			
Super Stars	1:80		$28
❏ Racing Champions ▲	1:64		$35
❏ Racing Champions DEI	1:87		$25
❏			

How Many: **Total Value:**

4

PHOTO UNAVAILABLE

Goodwrench – Busch Series
1994 Transporter

	Scale	LE	Value
❏ Action/Kenworth	1:64		$65
❏ Racing Champions	1:87		$80
❏			
❏			
❏			

How Many: **Total Value:**

5

7&7 Earnhardt/Petty
1995 Transporter

	Scale	LE	Value
❏ Action/Featherlite (7-time) ▲	1:64		$55
❏ Nylint Steel	1:25		$110
❏			
❏			

How Many: **Total Value:**

6

Goodwrench
1995 Transporter

	Scale	LE	Value
❏ Action/RCCA	1:96		N/E
❏ Brookfield			
Collector's Guild ▲	1:25		N/E
❏ Matchbox/White Rose			
Super Stars	1:80		$18
❏			

How Many: **Total Value:**

	How Many	Total Value
Page Totals:		

Transporters

1

PHOTO
UNAVAILABLE

Goodwrench – Snap On
1995 Transporter

	Scale	LE	Value
☐ Matchbox/White Rose			
Super Stars	1:80		$28
☐			
☐			
☐			

How Many: _____ **Total Value:** _____

2

Goodwrench Racing
1995 Transporter

	Scale	LE	Value
☐ Action/Featherlite ▲	1:64		N/E
☐			
☐			
☐			

How Many: _____ **Total Value:** _____

3

PHOTO
UNAVAILABLE

Winston Select
1995 Transporter

	Scale	LE	Value
☐ Nylint Steel (black trailer)	1:25		$175
☐ Nylint Steel (silver trailer)	1:25		$400
☐			
☐			
☐			

How Many: _____ **Total Value:** _____

4

PHOTO
UNAVAILABLE

Goodwrench
1996 Transporter

	Scale	LE	Value
☐ Peachstate	1:64		$100
☐			
☐			
☐			

How Many: _____ **Total Value:** _____

5

PHOTO
UNAVAILABLE

Bass Pro Shops
1998 Transporter

	Scale	LE	Value
☐ Brookfield			
Collector's Guild	1:25		$65
☐			
☐			
☐			

How Many: _____ **Total Value:** _____

6

PHOTO
UNAVAILABLE

Goodwrench Plus – Sign Car
1999 Transporter

	Scale	LE	Value
☐ Action	1:64		N/E
☐			
☐			
☐			

How Many: _____ **Total Value:** _____

Page Totals: | How Many _____ | Total Value _____

Collector's Value Guide™ – Dale Earnhardt®

PHOTO UNAVAILABLE

Taz No Bull 2000 Transporter

	Scale	LE	Value
☐ Brookfield			
Collector's Guild	1:24		$165
☐			
☐			
☐			

How Many: Total Value:

2

PHOTO UNAVAILABLE

RCCA Transporter

	Scale	LE	Value
☐ Action/RCCA ▲	1:64		$100
☐			
☐			
☐			

How Many: Total Value:

3

PHOTO UNAVAILABLE

Wrangler Transporter

	Scale	LE	Value
☐ Brookfield			
Collector's Guild	1:25		$85
☐ Nylint Steel	1:25		$100
☐			
☐			

How Many: Total Value:

4

Bass Pro Shops 1998 Van

	Scale	LE	Value
☐ Brookfield			
Collector's Guild ▲	1:25		N/E
☐			
☐			
☐			

How Many: Total Value:

Transporters/Vans

COLLECTOR'S VALUE GUIDE™

Page Totals:	How Many	Total Value

125

Trading Cards

With career statistics and facts, trading cards are as unique as the races each driver runs. Individual cards typically command greater secondary market values than card sets, as collectors may be willing to pay more for single cards that will complete their collections.

AC Racing

			Value
❑	1990	Proven Winners #3	$22.00
❑	1991	#1	N/E
❑	1992	Postcard #1	N/E
❑	1993	Foldout #3	N/E

Action Packed

			Value
❑	1993	#88	$4.00
❑	1993	#89 (car)	$1.50
❑	1993	#94	$3.00
❑	1993	#95	$3.00
❑	1993	#120	$2.00
❑	1993	#121	$2.00
❑	1993	#122	$2.00
❑	1993	#123	$2.00
❑	1993	#124 (Braille)	$2.00
❑	1993	#125 (Braille)	$2.00
❑	1993	#126 (Braille)	$2.00
❑	1993	#127 (Braille)	$2.00
❑	1993	#138	$2.00
❑	1993	#139	$2.00
❑	1993	#171	$2.25
❑	1993	#198	$2.00
❑	1993	#202	$2.00
❑	1993	#207	$2.00
❑	1993	24K Gold #18G	$90.00
❑	1993	24K Gold #19G	$90.00
❑	1993	24K Gold #20G	$90.00
❑	1993	24K Gold #21G	$90.00
❑	1993	24K Gold #22G (Braille)	$90.00
❑	1993	24K Gold #23G (Braille)	$90.00

1994 Action Packed #8

Action Packed, cont.

			Value
❑	1993	24K Gold #24G (Braille)	$90.00
❑	1993	24K Gold #25G (Braille)	$90.00
❑	1993	24K Gold #37G	$90.00
❑	1993	24K Gold #38G	$90.00
❑	1993	24K Gold #53G	$70.00
❑	1994	#1	$2.50
❑	1994	#8	$2.75
❑	1994	#32	$2.25
❑	1994	#41 (car)	$0.75
❑	1994	#68	$2.75
❑	1994	#99	$2.50
❑	1994	#104	$2.00
❑	1994	#126 (car)	$0.50
❑	1994	#179	$0.50
❑	1994	#180	$0.50
❑	1994	#187	$0.50
❑	1994	24K Gold #2G	$80.00
❑	1994	24K Gold #11G (car)	$40.00
❑	1994	24K Gold #22G	$80.00
❑	1994	24K Gold #179G	$70.00
❑	1994	24K Gold #180G	$70.00
❑	1994	24K Gold #187G	$70.00
❑	1994	Champ And Challenger #21	$0.65
❑	1994	Champ And Challenger #22	$0.65
❑	1994	Champ And Challenger #23	$0.65
❑	1994	Champ And Challenger #24	$0.65
❑	1994	Champ And Challenger #25	$0.65
❑	1994	Champ And Challenger #26	$0.65
❑	1994	Champ And Challenger #27	$0.65
❑	1994	Champ And Challenger #28	$0.65
❑	1994	Champ And Challenger #29	$0.65
❑	1994	Champ And Challenger #30	$0.65
❑	1994	Champ And Challenger #31	$0.65
❑	1994	Champ And Challenger #32 (car)	$0.65
❑	1994	Champ And Challenger #33 (car)	$0.65
❑	1994	Champ And Challenger #34 (car)	$0.65
❑	1994	Champ And Challenger #35 (car)	$0.65
❑	1994	Champ And Challenger #36 (car)	$0.65
❑	1994	Champ And Challenger #37 (car)	$0.65
❑	1994	Champ And Challenger #38	$0.65
❑	1994	Champ And Challenger #39	$0.65

Page Totals:	How Many	Total Value

1995 Action Packed Preview #59

Action Packed, cont.			Value
❏	1994	Champ And Challenger #40 . .	$0.65
❏	1994	Champ And Challenger #41 (car)	$0.65
❏	1994	Champ And Challenger #42 . .	$0.65
❏	1994	Champ And Challenger 24K Gold #22G	$40.00
❏	1994	Champ And Challenger 24K Gold #28G	$40.00
❏	1994	Champ And Challenger 24K Gold #30G	$40.00
❏	1994	Champ And Challenger 24K Gold #32G (car)	$40.00
❏	1994	Champ And Challenger 24K Gold #39G	$40.00
❏	1994	Champ And Challenger 24K Gold #41G (car)	$40.00
❏	1994	Champ And Challenger 24K Gold #42G	$40.00
❏	1994	Richard Childress Racing #RCR2 (car).	$0.70
❏	1994	Richard Childress Racing #RCR3.	$1.50
❏	1994	Richard Childress Racing #RCR4.	$1.50
❏	1994	Richard Childress Racing #RCR5 (car).	$0.70
❏	1994	Richard Childress Racing #RCR6 (car).	$0.70
❏	1994	Select 24K Gold #W3	$15.00
❏	1994	Select 24K Gold #W6	$15.00
❏	1994	Select 24KGold #W9	$15.00
❏	1995	Country #11.	$1.00
❏	1995	Country #17.	$1.00
❏	1995	Country #5	$0.75

Action Packed, cont.			Value
❏	1995	Country #25	$0.75
❏	1995	Country #26	$0.75
❏	1995	Country #27	$0.75
❏	1995	Country #28	$0.75
❏	1995	Country #29	$0.75
❏	1995	Country #30	$0.75
❏	1995	Country #31	$0.75
❏	1995	Country #45	$0.75
❏	1995	Country #54	$0.75
❏	1995	Country #62	$2.00
❏	1995	Country 24K Gold #5.	$55.00
❏	1995	Country 24K Gold #6.	$55.00
❏	1995	Country 24K Gold #7.	$55.00
❏	1995	Country Second Career Choice #6	$15.00
❏	1995	Country Silver Speed #25	$6.00
❏	1995	Mammoth #MM1	$3.00
❏	1995	Mammoth #MM6	$3.00
❏	1995	Preview #7	$1.75
❏	1995	Preview #33	$1.00
❏	1995	Preview #48	$1.00
❏	1995	Preview #59	$1.00
❏	1995	Preview #BP1	$15.00
❏	1995	Stars #23	$2.00
❏	1995	Stars #31 (car)	$0.85
❏	1995	Stars #52	$1.00
❏	1995	Stars 24K Gold #7G	$65.00
❏	1995	Stars 24K Gold #9G	$65.00
❏	1995	Stars 24K Gold #10G	$65.00
❏	1995	Stars 24K Gold #11G	$65.00
❏	1995	Stars 24K Gold #12G	$65.00
❏	1995	Stars 24K Gold #13G	$65.00
❏	1995	Stars 24K Gold #14G	$65.00
❏	1995	Stars 24K Gold #15G	$65.00
❏	1995	Stars 24K Gold #16G	$65.00
❏	1995	Stars Dale Earnhardt Race For Eight #DE1	$8.00
❏	1995	Stars Dale Earnhardt Race For Eight #DE2	$8.00
❏	1995	Stars Dale Earnhardt Race For Eight #DE3	$8.00
❏	1995	Stars Dale Earnhardt Race For Eight #DE4	$8.00
❏	1995	Stars Dale Earnhardt Race For Eight #DE5	$8.00
❏	1995	Stars Dale Earnhardt Race For Eight #DE6	$8.00
❏	1995	Stars Dale Earnhardt Race For Eight #DE7	$8.00
❏	1995	Stars Dale Earnhardt Race For Eight #DE8 (car)	$8.00
❏	1995	Stars Dale Earnhardt Race For Eight (set/8)	$75.00
❏	1995	Stars Dale Earnhardt Silver Salute #1	$8.00
❏	1995	Stars Dale Earnhardt Silver Salute #2	$8.00
❏	1995	Stars Dale Earnhardt Silver Salute #3 (car)	$65.00
❏	1995	Stars Dale Earnhardt Silver Salute #4	$65.00

Page Totals:	How Many	Total Value

Trading Cards

Action Packed, cont.		Value
1995	Stars Dale Earnhardt Silver Salute (set/4)	N/E
1995	Stars Silver Speed #23	$10.00
1995	Stars Silver Speed #31	$5.00
1995	Stars Silver Speed #52	$10.00
1995	Sundrop Dale Earnhardt #SD1	$4.00
1995	Sundrop Dale Earnhardt #SD2	$4.00
1995	Sundrop Dale Earnhardt #SD3	$6.50
1995	Sundrop Dale Earnhardt (set/3)	$13.00
1996	Credentials #6	$0.75
1996	Credentials #7	$0.75
1996	Credentials #8	$0.75
1996	Credentials #9	$0.75
1996	Credentials #10	$1.00
1996	Credentials #17	$1.00
1996	Credentials #21	$2.00
1996	Credentials #57	$1.00
1996	Credentials #104	$1.00
1996	Credentials Fan Scan #1	$65.00
1996	Credentials Fan Scan #2 (car)	$55.00
1996	Credentials Leaders Of The Pack #1	$20.00
1996	Credentials Leaders Of The Pack #2	$20.00
1996	Credentials Leaders Of The Pack #3	$20.00
1996	Credentials Leaders Of The Pack #4	$20.00
1996	Credentials Oversized #1	$6.75
1996	Credentials Silver Speed #6	$4.50
1996	Credentials Silver Speed #7	$4.50
1996	Credentials Silver Speed #8	$4.50
1996	Credentials Silver Speed #9	$4.50
1996	Credentials Silver Speed #10	$4.50
1996	Credentials Silver Speed #17	$4.00
1996	Credentials Silver Speed #21	$10.00
1996	McDonald's #2	$1.25
1996	McDonald's #12 (car)	$0.75
1997	24K Gold #2	$85.00

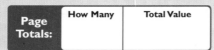

1996 Action Packed Credentials Fan Scan #2

Burger King

		Value
1998	#1 (car)	$1.75
1998	#2	$2.50
1998	#3 (car)	$1.75
1998	#4	$2.25
1998	set/4	$8.00

Card Dynamics

1992	Black Top Busch Series #1	$13.00
1993	Check #8	$15.00
1993	Double Edge Eagle Postcard #3	$130.00
1993	Gant Oil #8	$16.00
1993	North State Chevrolet #2	$100.00
1994	Double Eagle #1	$12.00
1994	Double Eagle #2	$12.00
1994	Double Eagle #3	$12.00
1994	Double Eagle #4	$12.00
1994	Double Eagle #5	$12.00
1994	Double Eagle #6	$12.00
1994	Double Eagle (set/6)	$65.00

Classic

1995	Assets #1	$2.00
1995	Assets #29	$2.00
1995	Assets #44	$2.00
1995	Assets #46 (car)	$1.00
1995	Assets Gold Signature #1	$16.00
1995	Assets Gold Signature #29	$16.00
1995	Assets Gold Signature #44	$16.00
1995	Assets Gold Signature #46 (car)	$15.00
1995	Assets Images Preview #RI1	$10.00
1995	Images #3	$2.00
1995	Images #50	$2.00
1995	Images #97	$2.00
1995	Images #99	$1.00
1995	Images Circuit Champions #8	$8.00
1995	Images Driven #D1	$3.25
1995	Images Gold #3	$2.50
1995	Images Gold #50	$2.50
1995	Images Gold #97	$2.50
1995	Images Gold #99	$1.25
1995	Images Hard Chargers #HC9	$3.00
1995	Images Owner's Pride #OP13	$3.00
1995	Images Race Reflections #DE1	$8.00
1995	Images Race Reflections #DE2	$8.00
1995	Images Race Reflections #DE3	$8.00
1995	Images Race Reflections #DE4	$8.00
1995	Images Race Reflections #DE5	$8.00
1995	Images Race Reflections #DE6	$8.00

Page Totals:	How Many	Total Value

COLLECTOR'S
VALUE GUIDE™

1995 Action Packed Stars #23

Classic cont.		Value
1995	Images Race Reflections #DE7	$8.00
1995	Images Race Reflections #DE8	$8.00
1995	Images Race Reflections #DE9	$8.00
1995	Images Race Reflections #DE10	$8.00
1995	Images Race Reflections (set/10)	$85.00
1995	Images Race Reflections Signature	N/E
1996	#32 (car)	$0.75
1996	#53	$8.00
1996	Assets #1	$2.00
1996	Assets #38	$2.00
1996	Assets #44	$2.00
1996	Assets Competitor's License #CL4	$22.00
1996	Assets Race Day #RD3	$17.00
1996	Autographed Racing #1	$1.25
1996	Autographed Racing #25 (car)	$0.75
1996	Autographed Racing Autographs #13	$150.00
1996	Autographed Racing Front Runners #13	$1.00
1996	Autographed Racing Front Runners #14	$1.00
1996	Autographed Racing Front Runners #15	$1.00
1996	Autographed Racing Front Runners #16	$1.00

Classic, cont.		Value
1996	Autographed Racing Front Runners #17	$1.00
1996	Autographed Racing Front Runners #18 (car)	$1.00
1996	Autographed Racing High Performance #HP1	$10.00
1996	Images Preview #RP5 (car)	$10.00
1996	InnerView #IV3	$13.00
1996	InnerView #IV7	$13.00
1996	Mark Martin's Challengers #MC3 (car)	$3.00
1996	Printer's Proof #32 (car)	$16.00
1996	Printer's Proof #53	$300.00
1996	Race Chase #RC3 (car)	$6.00
1996	Race Chase #RC13 (car)	$6.00
1996	Silver #32 (car)	$1.00
1996	Silver #53	$15.00

Dayco

1993	Series 2 Rusty Wallace #12	$1.00

Finish Line

1995	#1	$1.50
1995	#89	$1.50
1995	#111	$1.50
1995	Coca-Cola 600 #29	$1.00
1995	Coca-Cola 600 #44	$1.00
1995	Coca-Cola 600 #46	$1.00
1995	Coca-Cola 600 Diecuts #C1	$1.00
1995	Coca-Cola 600 Winners #CC2	$1.00
1995	Coca-Cola 600 Winners #CC8	$1.00
1995	Coca-Cola 600 Winners #CC9	$1.00
1995	Dale Earnhardt #DE1	$7.50
1995	Dale Earnhardt #DE2	$7.50
1995	Dale Earnhardt #DE3	$7.50
1995	Dale Earnhardt #DE4	$7.50
1995	Dale Earnhardt #DE5	$7.50
1995	Dale Earnhardt #DE6	$7.50
1995	Dale Earnhardt #DE7	$7.50
1995	Dale Earnhardt #DE8	$7.50
1995	Dale Earnhardt #DE9	$7.50
1995	Dale Earnhardt #DE10	$7.50
1995	Dale Earnhardt (set/10)	$175.00
1995	Dale Earnhardt Auto Blue #NNO	$230.00
1995	Dale Earnhardt Auto Red #NNO	$230.00
1995	Gold Signature #GS3	$10.00
1995	Printer's Proof #1	$25.00
1995	Printer's Proof #89	$25.00
1995	Printer's Proof #111	$25.00
1995	Silver #1	$6.00
1995	Silver #89	$6.00
1995	Silver #111	$6.00
1995	Standout Cars #SC1 (car)	$3.00
1995	Standout Drivers #SD1	$8.00

Page Totals:	How Many	Total Value

Trading Cards

		Value
	Flair	
❏	1996 #10	$2.50
❏	1996 #66 (car)	$1.00
❏	1996 Autographs #2	$235.00
❏	1996 Center Spotlight #2	$12.00
❏	1996 Hot Numbers #1	$50.00
❏	1996 Power Performance #2	$22.00
	Fleer	
❏	1996 Ultra #5	$1.50
❏	1996 Ultra #6	$1.50
❏	1996 Ultra #7 (car)	$0.75
❏	1996 Ultra #173	$0.75
❏	1996 Ultra #175 (car)	$0.75
❏	1996 Ultra #176	$0.75
❏	1996 Ultra #185	$0.75
❏	1996 Ultra #187 (car)	$0.75
❏	1996 Ultra #192	$0.75
❏	1996 Ultra #197	$0.75
❏	1996 Ultra #200 (car)	$0.75
❏	1996 Ultra Autographs #9	$245.00
❏	1996 Ultra Boxed Set #2	$5.00
❏	1996 Ultra Champions Club #2	$5.00
❏	1996 Ultra Flair Preview #2	$20.00
❏	1996 Ultra Golden Memories #4	$8.00
❏	1996 Ultra Season Crowns #3	$6.00
❏	1996 Ultra Season Crowns #5	$6.00
❏	1996 Ultra Season Crowns #9	$6.00
❏	1996 Ultra Season Crowns #12 (car)	$2.25
❏	1996 Ultra Season Crowns #15	$6.00
❏	1996 Ultra Thunder And Lightning #5 (car)	$5.00
❏	1996 Ultra Thunder And Lightning #6 (car)	$5.00
❏	1996 Ultra Update #7	$4.25
❏	1996 Ultra Update #10	$1.25
❏	1996 Ultra Update #16	$4.25
❏	1996 Ultra Update #45	$0.50
❏	1996 Ultra Update #56 (car)	$0.50
❏	1996 Ultra Update #96	$1.00
❏	1996 Ultra Update Autographs #2	$235.00

1996 Fleer Ultra Season Crowns #3

		Value
	Fleer, cont.	
❏	1996 Ultra Update Proven Power #2	$65.00
❏	1997 Ultra #10	$1.50
❏	1997 Ultra #43 (car)	$1.00
❏	1997 Ultra AKA #A1	$35.00
❏	1997 Ultra Inside/Out #DC1	$12.00
❏	1997 Ultra Shoney's #3	$2.50
❏	1997 Ultra Update #2	$2.25
❏	1997 Ultra Update #77 (car)	$1.00
❏	1997 Ultra Update Autographs #2	$190.00
❏	1997 Ultra Update Driver View #D6	$15.00
❏	1997 Ultra Update Elite Seats #E2	$22.00
	Hi-Tech	
❏	1993 Tire Test #1 (car)	$0.50
❏	1994 Brickyard 400 #9 (car)	$0.75
❏	1994 Brickyard 400 #38	$2.00
❏	1994 Brickyard 400 Artist's Proof #9 (car)	N/E
❏	1994 Brickyard 400 Artist's Proof #38	N/E
❏	1995 Brickyard 400 #2 (car)	$0.60
❏	1995 Brickyard 400 #41	$0.60
❏	1995 Brickyard 400 #56	$0.60
❏	1995 Brickyard 400 #77 (car)	$0.60
❏	1995 Brickyard 400 #87	$0.60
❏	1995 Brickyard 400 Top Ten Holofoils #BY5	$0.60
	Hickory Motor Speedway	
❏	1991 #6	$2.00
❏	1991 #10 (car)	$0.75
	Highland Mint	
❏	1994-1995 VIP Bronze #1B	$45.00
❏	1994-1995 VIP Gold #1G	$30.00
❏	1994-1995 VIP Silver #1S	$30.00
	IROC	
❏	1991 #12	$135.00
	Maxx	
❏	1988 Charlotte #9 (car)	$3.00
❏	1988 Charlotte #13 (car)	$3.00
❏	1988 Charlotte #17 (car)	$7.50
❏	1988 Charlotte #38	$7.00
❏	1988 Charlotte #45 (trailer)	$1.50
❏	1988 Charlotte #49 (car)	$3.50
❏	1988 Charlotte #54 (car)	$8.00
❏	1988 Charlotte #84 (car)	$2.75
❏	1988 Charlotte #87	$65.00
❏	1988 Charlotte #99	$2.50
❏	1989 #3	$75.00
❏	1989 #60	$10.00
❏	1989 #102 (car)	$8.00
❏	1989 #108 (car)	$5.00
❏	1989 #121 (car)	$5.00

Page Totals:	How Many	Total Value

COLLECTOR'S
VALUE GUIDE™

1995 Hi-Tech Brickyard 400 Top Ten
Holofoils #BY5

Maxx, cont.		Value
❑	1989 #144	$10.00
❑	1989 #148	$10.00
❑	1989 #160	$10.00
❑	1989 Crisco #6	$1.50
❑	1989 Stickers #3/52	$2.50
❑	1989 Stickers #15/3	$2.50
❑	1990 #3	$12.00
❑	1990 #116	$7.00
❑	1990 #179	$5.00
❑	1990 #183	$2.00
❑	1990 #191	$2.00
❑	1990 #195	$1.00
❑	1990 Holly Farms #HF1	$2.00
❑	1991 #3	$1.50
❑	1991 #173	$1.00
❑	1991 #174	$1.00
❑	1991 #178	$1.00
❑	1991 #179	$1.00
❑	1991 #184	$1.00
❑	1991 #185	$1.00
❑	1991 #187	$1.00
❑	1991 #191	$1.00
❑	1991 #192	$1.00
❑	1991 #198	$1.00
❑	1991 #200	$1.00
❑	1991 #220	$1.00
❑	1991 McDonald's #1A	$4.50
❑	1991 McDonald's #1B	$3.00
❑	1991 McDonald's #30	$0.50
❑	1991 Racing For Kids Sheet #1	$26.00
❑	1991 Update #3	$3.00
❑	1991 Update #200	$2.00

Maxx, cont.		Value
❑	1991 Update #220	$2.00
❑	1991 The Winston 20th Anniversary Foils #10	$1.50
❑	1991 The Winston 20th Anniversary Foils #16	$1.50
❑	1991 The Winston 20th Anniversary Foils #17	$1.50
❑	1991 The Winston 20th Anniversary Foils #20	$1.50
❑	1991 The Winston Acrylics #5	$1.25
❑	1992 All Pro Team #1	$1.75
❑	1992 Black #3	$3.00
❑	1992 Black #203 (car)	$1.50
❑	1992 Black #231	$1.50
❑	1992 Black #265	$1.50
❑	1992 Black #271	$1.50
❑	1992 Black #281	$1.50
❑	1992 Black #289	$1.50
❑	1992 Black #294	$1.50
❑	1992 McDonald's #1	$1.75
❑	1992 McDonald's #2	$1.75
❑	1992 Red #3	$1.50
❑	1992 Red #203 (car)	$0.75
❑	1992 Red #231	$0.75
❑	1992 Red #265	$0.75
❑	1992 Red #271	$0.75
❑	1992 Red #281	$0.75
❑	1992 Red #289	$0.75
❑	1992 Red #294	$0.75
❑	1992 Texaco Davey Allison #12 (car)	$0.50
❑	1992 The Winston #14	$1.75
❑	1992 The Winston #34 (car)	$1.00
❑	1993 #3	$1.50
❑	1993 #56 (car)	$0.50
❑	1993 #274 (car)	$1.00
❑	1993 Premier #3	$3.00
❑	1993 Premier #56 (car)	$1.00
❑	1993 Premier #274 (car)	$1.50
❑	1993 Premier Plus #3	$3.00
❑	1993 Premier Plus #56 (car)	$0.75
❑	1993 Premier Plus #189	$3.00
❑	1993 Premier Plus Error	N/E
❑	1993 Premier Plus Jumbos #NNO	$12.00
❑	1993 The Winston #1	$0.75
❑	1993 The Winston #21 (car)	$0.50
❑	1993 The Winston #49 (car)	$0.50
❑	1993 The Winston #50	$0.75
❑	1993 The Winston Chromium #51	$1.75
❑	1993 Year In Review #274	N/E
❑	1994 #3	$2.00
❑	1994 #23 (car)	$1.00
❑	1994 #211	$1.00
❑	1994 #218	$1.00
❑	1994 #219	$1.00
❑	1994 #222	$2.00
❑	1994 #224	$1.00
❑	1994 #225	$1.00
❑	1994 #238	$1.25
❑	1994 #334 (car)	$0.50
❑	1994 #335 (car)	$0.75

Page Totals:	How Many	Total Value

Trading Cards

Maxx, cont.		Value
❏	1994 Medallion #46	$1.00
❏	1994 Medallion #99SP	$380.00
❏	1994 Premier #3	$3.00
❏	1994 Premier #23 (car)	$0.75
❏	1994 Premier #270	$2.00
❏	1994 Premier #277	$2.00
❏	1994 Premier #278	$2.00
❏	1994 Premier #281	$2.00
❏	1994 Premier #283	$2.00
❏	1994 Premier #284	$2.00
❏	1994 Premier #297	$3.00
❏	1994 Premier Plus #3	N/E
❏	1994 Premier Plus #23 (car)	$1.25
❏	1994 Premier Plus #165	$1.25
❏	1994 Premier Plus #170	$1.25
❏	1994 Premier Plus #177	$1.25
❏	1994 Premier Plus #178	$1.25
❏	1994 Premier Plus #181	$1.25
❏	1994 Premier Plus #183	$1.25
❏	1994 Premier Plus #184	$1.25
❏	1994 Rookies Of The Year #3	$9.00
❏	1994 The Winston Select 25 #1	$5.00
❏	1995 Chase The Champion #1	$7.00
❏	1995 Chase The Champion #2	$8.00
❏	1995 Chase The Champion #3	$8.00
❏	1995 Chase The Champion #4 (car)	$8.00
❏	1995 Chase The Champion #5	$8.00
❏	1995 Chase The Champion #6	$7.00
❏	1995 Chase The Champion #7	$7.00
❏	1995 Chase The Champion #8	$8.00
❏	1995 Chase The Champion #9	$8.00
❏	1995 Chase The Champion #10	$8.00
❏	1995 Crown Chrome Silver Select #NNO	N/E
❏	1995 Dale Earnhardt Larger Than Life #1	$4.00
❏	1995 Dale Earnhardt Larger Than Life #2	$4.00
❏	1995 Dale Earnhardt Larger Than Life #3	$4.00
❏	1995 Dale Earnhardt Larger Than Life #4	$4.00
❏	1995 Dale Earnhardt Larger Than Life #5	$4.00

Maxx, cont.		Value
❏	1995 Dale Earnhardt Larger Than Life #6	$4.00
❏	1995 Dale Earnhardt Larger Than Life #7	$4.00
❏	1995 Dale Earnhardt Larger Than Life (set/7)	$20.00
❏	1995 Premier Plus Silver Select	$100.00
❏	1996 #3	$1.25
❏	1996 Odyssey Millennium #MM1	$2.25
❏	1996 Premier #3	$3.00
❏	1996 Premier #73 (car)	$1.75
❏	1996 Premier #262	$1.75
❏	1997 #3	$1.25
❏	1997 #48 (car)	$0.75
❏	1997 Flag Firsts #FF14	$10.00
❏	1998 10th Anniversary #96	$2.25
❏	1998 10th Anniversary #119	$2.00
❏	1998 10th Anniversary Champions Past #CP3	$10.00
❏	1998 10th Anniversary Champions Past Diecuts #CP3	$40.00
❏	1998 #3	$1.25
❏	1998 #33 (car)	$0.75
❏	1998 #95 (car)	$0.75
❏	1998 Focus On A Champion #FC3	$18.00
❏	1998 Focus On A Champion Cel #FC3	$4.00
❏	1998 Year In Review #9 (car)	$0.50
❏	1998 Year In Review #33 (car)	$0.50
❏	1998 Year In Review #53 (car)	$0.50
❏	1998 Year In Review #128 (car)	$0.50
❏	1998 Year In Review #PO5	$3.00
❏	1999 #88	$2.00
❏	1999 #89 (car)	$1.00
❏	1999 Fanastic Finishes #F10 (car)	$14.00
❏	1999 Focus On A Champion #FC2	$8.00
❏	1999 Focus On A Champion Gold #FC2	$25.00
❏	1999 Race Ticket #RT4 (car)	N/E

Maxximum

		Value
❏	1998 #3	$3.00
❏	1998 #28 (car)	$1.50
❏	1998 Battle Proven #B2	$7.00
❏	1998 Field Generals Four Star Star Autographs #10	N/E
❏	1998 Field Generals One Star #10	N/E
❏	1998 Field Generals Three Star Autographs #10	$235.00
❏	1998 Field Generals Two Star #10	N/E

Metallic Impressions

		Value
❏	1995 Classic Dale Earnhardt #1	$1.25
❏	1995 Classic Dale Earnhardt #2	$1.25
❏	1995 Classic Dale Earnhardt #3	$1.25
❏	1995 Classic Dale Earnhardt #4	$1.25
❏	1995 Classic Dale Earnhardt #5	$1.25

1996 Maxx Odyssey Millennium #MM1

Page Totals:	How Many	Total Value

COLLECTOR'S
VALUE GUIDE™

1997 Pinnacle Racing #70

Metallic Impressions, cont.

			Value
❏	1995	Classic Dale Earnhardt #6	$1.25
❏	1995	Classic Dale Earnhardt #7	$1.25
❏	1995	Classic Dale Earnhardt #8	$1.25
❏	1995	Classic Dale Earnhardt #9	$1.25
❏	1995	Classic Dale Earnhardt #10	$1.25
❏	1995	Classic Dale Earnhardt #11	$1.25
❏	1995	Classic Dale Earnhardt #12	$1.25
❏	1995	Classic Dale Earnhardt #13	$1.25
❏	1995	Classic Dale Earnhardt #14	$1.25
❏	1995	Classic Dale Earnhardt #15	$1.25
❏	1995	Classic Dale Earnhardt #16	$1.25
❏	1995	Classic Dale Earnhardt #17	$1.25
❏	1995	Classic Dale Earnhardt #18	$1.25
❏	1995	Classic Dale Earnhardt #19	$1.25
❏	1995	Classic Dale Earnhardt #20	$1.25
❏	1995	Classic Dale Earnhardt #E1	$1.25
❏	1995	Classic Dale Earnhardt (set/21)	N/E
❏	1995	Winston Cup Champions #4	$8.00
❏	1996	25th Anniversary Winston Cup Champions #10	$3.00
❏	1996	25th Anniversary Winston Cup Champions #16	$3.00
❏	1996	25th Anniversary Winston Cup Champions #17	$3.00
❏	1996	25th Anniversary Winston Cup Champions #20	$3.00
❏	1996	25th Anniversary Winston Cup Champions #21	$3.00
❏	1996	25th Anniversary Winston Cup Champions #23	$3.00
❏	1996	25th Anniversary Winston Cup Champions #24	$3.00

Metallic Impressions, cont.

			Value
❏	1996	Avon All-Time Racing Greatest #1	$6.00
❏	1996	Winston Cup Top 5 #4	$3.00

Pinnacle

			Value
❏	1995	Select #41 (car)	$1.00
❏	1995	Select #151S	$7.00
❏	1995	Select Dealer #151	$8.00
❏	1995	Select Flat Out #FO41	$7.00
❏	1995	Select Flat Out #FO151	$16.00
❏	1995	Zenith #3	$3.00
❏	1995	Zenith #36 (transporter)	$1.25
❏	1995	Zenith #76	$1.50
❏	1995	Zenith Helmets #1	$100.00
❏	1995	Zenith Tribute #1	$75.00
❏	1995	Zenith Winston Winners #7	$10.00
❏	1995	Zenith Winston Winners #10	$10.00
❏	1995	Zenith Winston Winners #19	$10.00
❏	1995	Zenith Winston Winners #24	$10.00
❏	1995	Zenith Z-Team #1	$80.00
❏	1996	#3	$1.75
❏	1996	#38 (car)	$0.75
❏	1996	#91 (transporter)	$0.75
❏	1996	Artist's Proof #3	$55.00
❏	1996	Artist's Proof #38 (car)	$15.00
❏	1996	Artist's Proof #91 (transporter)	$15.00
❏	1996	Checkered Flag #3	$15.00
❏	1996	Pole Position #3	$2.25
❏	1996	Pole Position #27 (car)	$1.00
❏	1996	Pole Position #56	$1.25
❏	1996	Pole Position #57	$1.25
❏	1996	Pole Position #58	$1.25
❏	1996	Pole Position #59	$1.25
❏	1996	Pole Position #60	$1.25
❏	1996	Pole Position #72	$1.25
❏	1996	Pole Position Certified Strong #3	$28.00
❏	1996	Pole Position Lightning Fast #3	$13.00
❏	1996	Pole Position Lightning Fast #27	$6.75
❏	1996	Pole Position Lightning Fast #56	$7.00
❏	1996	Pole Position Lightning Fast #57	$7.00
❏	1996	Pole Position Lightning Fast #58	$7.00
❏	1996	Pole Position Lightning Fast #59	$7.00
❏	1996	Pole Position Lightning Fast #60	$7.00
❏	1996	Pole Position Lightning Fast #72	$7.00
❏	1996	Pole Position No Limit #3	$45.00
❏	1996	Racer's Choice #3	$1.25
❏	1996	Racer's Choice #27 (car)	$0.75

Page Totals:	How Many	Total Value

Trading Cards

	Pinnacle, cont.	Value
❑	1996 Racer's Choice #56	$0.75
❑	1996 Racer's Choice #57	$0.75
❑	1996 Racer's Choice #58	$0.75
❑	1996 Racer's Choice #59	$0.75
❑	1996 Racer's Choice #60	$0.75
❑	1996 Racer's Choice #84	$0.75
❑	1996 Racer's Choice #89	$0.75
❑	1996 Racer's Choice #92	$0.75
❑	1996 Racer's Choice Artist's Proof #3	$20.00
❑	1996 Racer's Choice Artist's Proof #27 (car)	$9.00
❑	1996 Racer's Choice Artist's Proof #56	$9.00
❑	1996 Racer's Choice Artist's Proof #57	$9.00
❑	1996 Racer's Choice Artist's Proof #58	$9.00
❑	1996 Racer's Choice Artist's Proof #59	$9.00
❑	1996 Racer's Choice Artist's Proof #60	$9.00
❑	1996 Racer's Choice Artist's Proof #84	$9.00
❑	1996 Racer's Choice Artist's Proof #92	$9.00
❑	1996 Racer's Choice Speedway Collection #3	$4.00
❑	1996 Racer's Choice Speedway Collection #27 (car)	$1.50
❑	1996 Racer's Choice Speedway Collection #56	$4.00
❑	1996 Racer's Choice Speedway Collection #57	$4.00
❑	1996 Racer's Choice Speedway Collection #58	$4.00
❑	1996 Racer's Choice Speedway Collection #59	$4.00
❑	1996 Racer's Choice Speedway Collection #60	$2.25
❑	1996 Racer's Choice Speedway Collection #84	$2.25
❑	1996 Racer's Choice Speedway Collection #92	$2.25

1997 Pinnacle Racing #95

	Pinnacle, cont.	Value
❑	1996 Racer's Choice Sundrop #SD1	$4.00
❑	1996 Racer's Choice Sundrop #SD2	$4.00
❑	1996 Racer's Choice Sundrop #SD3	$4.00
❑	1996 Racer's Choice Sundrop (set/3)	$12.00
❑	1996 Racer's Choice Top Ten #2	$22.00
❑	1996 Racer's Choice Up Close With Dale Earnhardt #1	$6.00
❑	1996 Racer's Choice Up Close With Dale Earnhardt #2	$6.00
❑	1996 Racer's Choice Up Close With Dale Earnhardt #3	$6.00
❑	1996 Racer's Choice Up Close With Dale Earnhardt #4	$6.00
❑	1996 Racer's Choice Up Close With Dale Earnhardt #5	$6.00
❑	1996 Racer's Choice Up Close With Dale Earnhardt #6	$6.00
❑	1996 Racer's Choice Up Close With Dale Earnhardt #7	$6.00
❑	1996 Racer's Choice Up Close With Dale Earnhardt (set/7)	$40.00
❑	1996 SpeedFlix #17	$1.50
❑	1996 SpeedFlix #37	$0.75
❑	1996 SpeedFlix #51	$0.75
❑	1996 SpeedFlix #52	$0.75
❑	1996 SpeedFlix #53	$0.75
❑	1996 SpeedFlix #54	$0.75
❑	1996 SpeedFlix #83	$0.75
❑	1996 SpeedFlix #85	$0.75
❑	1996 SpeedFlix Artist's Proof #17	$20.00
❑	1996 SpeedFlix Artist's Proof #37	$10.00
❑	1996 SpeedFlix Artist's Proof #51	$10.00
❑	1996 SpeedFlix Artist's Proof #52	$10.00
❑	1996 SpeedFlix Artist's Proof #53	$10.00
❑	1996 SpeedFlix Artist's Proof #54	$10.00
❑	1996 SpeedFlix Artist's Proof #83	$13.00
❑	1996 SpeedFlix Artist's Proof #85	$13.00
❑	1996 SpeedFlix Clear Shots #1	$30.00
❑	1996 SpeedFlix In Motion #1 (helmet)	$22.00
❑	1996 SpeedFlix ProMotion #1	$10.00
❑	1996 Team #3	$75.00
❑	1996 Team #11	$75.00
❑	1996 Winston Cup Collection #3	$10.00
❑	1996 Winston Cup Collection #38 (car)	$4.50
❑	1996 Winston Cup Collection #91 (transporter)	$4.50
❑	1996 Zenith #1	$3.00
❑	1996 Zenith #35 (car)	$1.25
❑	1996 Zenith #50	$1.50
❑	1996 Zenith #65	$1.50
❑	1996 Zenith #66	$1.50
❑	1996 Zenith #67	$1.50
❑	1996 Zenith #68	$1.50
❑	1996 Zenith #69	$1.50
❑	1996 Zenith Artist's Proof #1	$75.00

Page Totals:

How Many | Total Value

COLLECTOR'S
VALUE GUIDE™

1998 Pinnacle Racer's Choice #89

Pinnacle, cont.

			Value
❏	1996	Zenith Artist's Proof #35 (car)	$35.00
❏	1996	Zenith Artist's Proof #50	$35.00
❏	1996	Zenith Artist's Proof #65	$35.00
❏	1996	Zenith Artist's Proof #66	$35.00
❏	1996	Zenith Artist's Proof #67	$35.00
❏	1996	Zenith Artist's Proof #68	$35.00
❏	1996	Zenith Artist's Proof #69	$35.00
❏	1996	Zenith Champion Salute #2	$110.00
❏	1996	Zenith Champion Salute #3	$110.00
❏	1996	Zenith Champion Salute #5	$110.00
❏	1996	Zenith Champion Salute #6	$110.00
❏	1996	Zenith Champion Salute #9	$110.00
❏	1996	Zenith Champion Salute #10	$110.00
❏	1996	Zenith Champion Salute #16	$110.00
❏	1996	Zenith Highlights #1	$15.00
❏	1996	Zenith Seven Wonders #1	$650.00
❏	1997	Action Packed First Impressions #3	N/E
❏	1997	Action Packed First Impressions #45	N/E
❏	1997	Action Packed First Impressions #84	N/E
❏	1997	Action Packed Racing #3	$2.00
❏	1997	Action Packed Racing #45 (car)	$1.00

Pinnacle, cont.

			Value
❏	1997	Action Packed Racing #84 (car)	$1.00
❏	1997	Action Packed Racing 24K Gold #2	$85.00
❏	1997	Action Packed Racing Chevy Madness #1 (car)	$10.00
❏	1997	Action Packed Racing Fifth Anniversary #6	$110.00
❏	1997	Action Packed Racing Rolling Thunder #2	$35.00
❏	1997	Certified #3	N/E
❏	1997	Certified #37 (car)	$2.00
❏	1997	Certified #76 (car)	$2.00
❏	1997	Certified #93	$2.00
❏	1997	Certified Epix #E1	N/E
❏	1997	Certified Epix Emerald #1	N/E
❏	1997	Certified Epix Purple #1	N/E
❏	1997	Certified Mirror Blue #3	$75.00
❏	1997	Certified Mirror Blue #37 (car)	$40.00
❏	1997	Certified Mirror Blue #76 (car)	$40.00
❏	1997	Certified Mirror Blue #93	$25.00
❏	1997	Certified Mirror Gold #3	$275.00
❏	1997	Certified Mirror Gold #37 (car)	$115.00
❏	1997	Certified Mirror Gold #76 (car)	$115.00
❏	1997	Certified Mirror Gold #93	$115.00
❏	1997	Certified Mirror Red #3	$40.00
❏	1997	Certified Mirror Red #37 (car)	$15.00
❏	1997	Certified Mirror Red #76 (car)	$20.00
❏	1997	Certified Mirror Red #93	$20.00
❏	1997	Certified Red #3	$25.00
❏	1997	Certified Red #37 (car)	$15.00
❏	1997	Certified Red #76 (car)	$14.00
❏	1997	Certified Red #93	$15.00
❏	1997	Certified Team #1	$30.00
❏	1997	Certified Team Gold #1	N/E
❏	1997	Mint Collection Bronze #21 (car)	$1.50
❏	1997	Mint Collection Diecuts #21 (car)	$2.00
❏	1997	Mint Collection Gold #21 (car)	$5.00
❏	1997	Mint Collection Mint Coins #21 (car)	$3.50
❏	1997	Mint Collection Silver #21 (car)	$3.00
❏	1997	Precision #12 (transporter)	$3.00
❏	1997	Precision #13	$3.00
❏	1997	Precision #14 (car)	$3.00
❏	1997	Precision #15	$7.00
❏	1997	Precision #17 (car)	$3.00
❏	1997	Precision #18	$7.00
❏	1997	Precision Bronze #12 (transporter)	$12.00
❏	1997	Precision Bronze #13	$12.00
❏	1997	Precision Bronze #14 (car)	$12.00

Trading Cards

COLLECTOR'S VALUE GUIDE™

Page Totals:	How Many	Total Value

Pinnacle, cont.	Value
1997 Precision Bronze #15	$35.00
1997 Precision Bronze #17 (car)	$12.00
1997 Precision Bronze #18	$35.00
1997 Precision Gold #12 (transporter)	$100.00
1997 Precision Gold #13	$100.00
1997 Precision Gold #14 (car)	$110.00
1997 Precision Gold #15	$230.00
1997 Precision Gold #17 (car)	$110.00
1997 Precision Gold #18	$225.00
1997 Precision Silver #12 (transporter)	$45.00
1997 Precision Silver #13	$45.00
1997 Precision Silver #14 (car)	$45.00
1997 Precision Silver #15	$60.00
1997 Precision Silver #17 (car)	$33.00
1997 Precision Silver #18	$60.00
1997 Racer's Choice #3	$1.25
1997 Racer's Choice #27	$1.50
1997 Racer's Choice #38 (car)	$0.50
1997 Racer's Choice #62 (car)	$0.50
1997 Racer's Choice #90	$0.50
1997 Racer's Choice #104	$0.75
1997 Racer's Choice #106	$0.75
1997 Racer's Choice Busch Clash #1	$35.00
1997 Racer's Choice Busch Clash #11	$35.00
1997 Racer's Choice Chevy Madness #8	$14.00
1997 Racer's Choice High Octane #2	$22.00
1997 Racer's Choice High Octane #15	$22.00
1997 Racer's Choice High Octane Glow In The Dark #2	$35.00
1997 Racer's Choice High Octane Glow In The Dark #15	$35.00
1997 Racer's Choice Showcase #3	$8.00
1997 Racer's Choice Showcase #38 (car)	$4.00
1997 Racer's Choice Showcase #62 (car)	$4.00

1997 Pinnacle Racing Chevy Madness #13

Pinnacle, cont.	Value
1997 Racer's Choice Showcase #90	$4.00
1997 Racer's Choice Showcase #104	$4.00
1997 Racer's Choice Showcase #106	$4.00
1997 Racing #3	$2.00
1997 Racing #32 (car)	$0.75
1997 Racing #66 (car)	$0.75
1997 Racing #68 (car)	$0.75
1997 Racing #69	$0.75
1997 Racing #70 (car)	$0.75
1997 Racing #82	$0.75
1997 Racing #84	$1.00
1997 Racing #91 (car)	$0.75
1997 Racing #95 (car)	$0.75
1997 Racing Artist's Proof Blue #32 (car)	$30.00
1997 Racing Artist's Proof Purple #3	$140.00
1997 Racing Artist's Proof Red #66 (car)	$10.00
1997 Racing Artist's Proof Red #68 (car)	$10.00
1997 Racing Artist's Proof Red #69	$10.00
1997 Racing Artist's Proof Red #70	$10.00
1997 Racing Artist's Proof Red #82	$10.00
1997 Racing Artist's Proof Red #84	$10.00
1997 Racing Artist's Proof Red #91 (car)	$10.00
1997 Racing Artist's Proof Red #95 (car)	$10.00
1997 Racing Chevy Madness #13 (car)	$20.00
1997 Racing Helmets #3S	N/E
1997 Racing Spellbound #3S	$26.00
1997 Racing Spellbound Autographs #3S	$215.00
1997 Racing Team #1	N/E
1997 Racing Team #3	$140.00
1997 Team Blue #3	$140.00
1997 Team Red #3	$140.00
1997 Totally Certified Platinum Blue #3	$17.00
1997 Totally Certified Platinum Blue #37 (car)	$8.00
1997 Totally Certified Platinum Blue #76	$8.00
1997 Totally Certified Platinum Blue #93	$8.00
1997 Totally Certified Platinum Gold #3	N/E
1997 Totally Certified Platinum Gold #37 (car)	N/E
1997 Totally Certified Platinum Gold #76	N/E

Page Totals:	How Many	Total Value

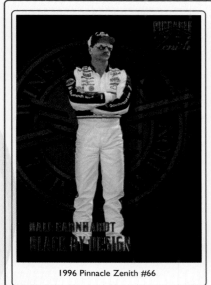

1996 Pinnacle Zenith #66

Pinnacle, cont.			Value
❏	1997	Totally Certified Platinum Gold #93	N/E
❏	1997	Totally Certified Platinum Red #3	$7.00
❏	1997	Totally Certified Platinum Red #37 (car)	$4.00
❏	1997	Totally Certified Platinum Red #76	$4.00
❏	1997	Totally Certified Platinum Red #93	$4.00
❏	1997	Trophy Collection #3	$1.00
❏	1997	Trophy Collection #32 (car)	$1.00
❏	1997	Trophy Collection #66 (car)	$1.00
❏	1997	Trophy Collection #68 (car)	$1.00
❏	1997	Trophy Collection #69	$1.00
❏	1997	Trophy Collection #70 (car)	$1.00
❏	1997	Trophy Collection #82	$1.00
❏	1997	Trophy Collection #84	$1.00
❏	1997	Trophy Collection #91 (car)	$1.00
❏	1997	Trophy Collection #95 (car)	$1.00
❏	1998	Mint #3	N/E
❏	1998	Mint #17	N/E
❏	1998	Mint Bronze #3	N/E
❏	1998	Mint Bronze #17	N/E
❏	1998	Mint Bronze Coins #3	N/E
❏	1998	Mint Bronze Coins #17	N/E
❏	1998	Mint Bronze-Plated Proof Coins #3	N/E
❏	1998	Mint Bronze-Plated Proof Coins #17	N/E
❏	1998	Mint Coins #3	N/E
❏	1998	Mint Coins #17 (car)	N/E
❏	1998	Mint Diecuts #3	N/E

Pinnacle, cont.			Value
❏	1998	Mint Diecuts Card #17	N/E
❏	1998	Mint Gold #3	N/E
❏	1998	Mint Gold #17	N/E
❏	1998	Mint Silver #3	N/E
❏	1998	Mint Silver #17	N/E
❏	1998	Mint Gold-Plated Coins #3	N/E
❏	1998	Mint Gold-Plated Coins #17	N/E
❏	1998	Mint Nickel-Silver Coins #3	N/E
❏	1998	Mint Nickel-Silver Coins #17	N/E
❏	1998	Mint Silver-Plated Proof Coins #3	N/E
❏	1998	Mint Silver-Plated Proof Coins #17	N/E
❏	1998	Mint Solid Gold Coins #3	N/E
❏	1998	Mint Solid Gold Coins #17	N/E
❏	1998	Mint Solid Silver Coins #3	N/E
❏	1998	Mint Solid Silver Coins #17	N/E

Press Pass

			Value
❏	1994	#5	$1.25
❏	1994	Checkered Flag #CF1	$3.50
❏	1994	Cup Chase #CC5	$40.00
❏	1994	Cup Chase Prize #SPCL1	$28.00
❏	1994	Holofoil #H1	$3.00
❏	1994	Optima XL #4	$2.25
❏	1994	Optima XL #41 (car)	$0.75
❏	1994	Optima XL #43B	$120.00
❏	1994	Optima XL Double Clutch #DC1	$15.00
❏	1994	Optima XL Red Hot #4.	$12.00
❏	1994	Optima XL Red Hot #41 (car)	$5.00
❏	1994	Optima XL Red Hot #43B.	$110.00
❏	1994	Race Day #RD10	$7.00
❏	1994	VIP #10	$2.25
❏	1994	VIP #42	$1.00
❏	1994	VIP Driver's Choice #DC1	$6.00
❏	1994	VIP Signature Exchange #EC1	$77.00
❏	1995	#9	$1.25
❏	1995	#41 (car)	$0.75
❏	1995	#115 (car)	$0.75
❏	1995	Checkered Flag #CF2	$6.00
❏	1995	Cup Chase #9	$22.00
❏	1995	Cup Chase Redemption #CCR2	$35.00
❏	1995	Optima XL #6	$2.25
❏	1995	Optima XL #51 (car)	$1.00
❏	1995	Optima XL Cool Blue #6.	$6.50
❏	1995	Optima XL Cool Blue #51 (car)	$2.25
❏	1995	Optima XL Diecut #6	$65.00
❏	1995	Optima XL Diecut #51 (car)	$10.00
❏	1995	Optima XL Red Hot #6.	$6.00
❏	1995	Optima XL Red Hot #51 (car).	$2.00
❏	1995	Optima XL Stealth #XLS2	$26.00
❏	1995	Premium #1	$3.00
❏	1995	Premium Holofoil #1	$7.00
❏	1995	Premium Hot Pursuit #HP2	$28.00
❏	1995	Premium Red Hot #1	$25.00

Page Totals:	How Many	Total Value

Trading Cards

Press Pass, cont.	Value
1995 Race Day #RD3	$18.00
1995 Red Hot #9	$10.00
1995 Red Hot #41 (car)	$6.00
1995 Red Hot #115 (car)	$6.00
1995 VIP #9	$2.25
1995 VIP Cool Blue #9	$8.00
1995 VIP Emerald Proof #9	$80.00
1995 VIP Fan's Choice #FC1	$10.00
1995 VIP Fan's Choice Gold #FC1	$85.00
1995 VIP Red Hot #9	$10.00
1996 #9	$1.25
1996 #40 (car)	$0.75
1996 Burning Rubber #BR3	$230.00
1996 Burning Rubber II #BR5	$240.00
1996 Cup Chase #9	$25.00
1996 Fastest Qualifying Speed #FQS1A	$15.00
1996 Fastest Qualifying Speed #FQS1B (car)	$5.00
1996 Focused #F1	$40.00
1996 M-Force #3	$3.50
1996 M-Force #4 (car)	$1.75
1996 M-Force #45 (car)	$1.75
1996 M-Force Black #B3	$3.50
1996 M-Force Black #B4 (car)	$1.75
1996 M-Force Sheet Metal #M2	$315.00
1996 M-Force Silver #S2	$22.00
1996 M-Force Silver #S3 (car)	$8.00
1996 Premium #2	$2.50
1996 Premium #35	$1.25
1996 Premium Crystal Ball #CB3	$30.00
1996 Premium Emerald Proof #2	$70.00
1996 Premium Emerald Proof #35 (car)	$30.00
1996 Premium Holofoil #2	$5.50
1996 Premium Holofoil #35 (car)	$3.00
1996 Premium Hot Pursuit #HP1	$30.00
1996 Scorchers #9	$7.00
1996 Scorchers #40 (car)	$3.00
1996 Torquers #40 (car)	$2.25
1996 Torquers #9	$4.00
1996 VIP #8	$2.00
1996 VIP #38 (car)	$1.50
1996 VIP Autographs #6	$200.00
1996 VIP Emerald Proof #8	$40.00

1996 Press Pass VIP #8

Press Pass, cont.	Value
1996 VIP Emerald Proof #38 (car)	$40.00
1996 VIP Fire Suit Blue #DE1	$435.00
1996 VIP Fire Suit Blue #DE2	$440.00
1996 VIP Fire Suit Gold #DE1	$230.00
1996 VIP Fire Suit Gold #DE2	$230.00
1996 VIP Fire Suit Green #DE1	$550.00
1996 VIP Fire Suit Green #DE2	$550.00
1996 VIP Fire Suit Silver #DE1	$400.00
1996 VIP Fire Suit Silver #DE2	$400.00
1996 VIP Head Gear #HG2	$20.00
1996 VIP Head Gear Diecuts #HG2	$275.00
1996 VIP Sam Bass Top Flight #SB1	$50.00
1996 VIP Sam Bass Top Flight Gold #SB1	N/E
1996 VIP Torquers #8	$4.75
1996 VIP Torquers #38 (car)	$2.00
1996 VIP War Paint #WP2 (car)	$20.00
1996 VIP War Paint Gold #WP2 (car)	N/E
1997 #4	$2.50
1997 #32 (car)	$1.00
1997 #56 (car)	$1.00
1997 #95 (car)	$1.00
1997 ActionVision #3	$7.00
1997 ActionVision #8	$7.00
1997 ActionVision Autographs #NNO	$250.00
1997 ActionVision Metal #6	$285.00
1997 Autographs #4	$250.00
1997 Banquet Bound #BB4	$10.00
1997 Burning Rubber #BR2	$240.00
1997 Clear Cut #C1	$18.00
1997 Cup Chase #CC5	$35.00
1997 Lasers #4	$4.00
1997 Lasers #32 (car)	$2.25
1997 Lasers #56 (car)	$2.25
1997 Lasers #95 (car)	$2.25
1997 Oil Slicks #4	$80.00
1997 Oil Slicks #32 (car)	$45.00
1997 Oil Slicks #56 (car)	$45.00
1997 Oil Slicks #95 (car)	$45.00
1997 Premium #4	$2.00
1997 Premium #29 (car)	$1.25
1997 Premium Autographs	N/E
1997 Premium Crystal Ball #CB2 (car)	$18.00
1997 Premium Crystal Ball Diecut #CB2 (car)	$26.00
1997 Premium Double Burners #DB1	$310.00
1997 Premium Emerald Proof #4	$70.00
1997 Premium Emerald Proof #29 (car)	$30.00
1997 Premium Lap Leaders #LL1	$15.00
1997 Premium Mirrors #29 (car)	$1.00
1997 Premium Mirrors #4	$6.00
1997 Premium Oil Slicks #4	$115.00
1997 Premium Oil Slicks #29 (car)	$50.00
1997 Torquers #4	$5.00

Page Totals: How Many | Total Value

COLLECTOR'S VALUE GUIDE™

1994 Press Pass Checkered Flag #CF1

Press Pass, cont.

			Value
❏	1997	Torquers #32 (car)	$2.25
❏	1997	Torquers #56 (car)	$2.25
❏	1997	Torquers #95 (car)	$2.25
❏	1997	Victory Lane #VL1A	$20.00
❏	1997	Victory Lane #VL1B (car)	$10.00
❏	1997	VIP #6	$3.00
❏	1997	VIP Explosives #6	$8.00
❏	1997	VIP Head Gear #HG1	$18.00
❏	1997	VIP Head Gear Diecuts #HG1	$30.00
❏	1997	VIP Knights Of Thunder #KT1	$30.00
❏	1997	VIP Knights Of Thunder Gold #KT1	$60.00
❏	1997	VIP Oil Slicks #6	$110.00
❏	1997	VIP Ring Of Honor #RH2 (car)	$16.00
❏	1997	VIP Ring Of Honor Diecuts #RH2 (car)	$28.00
❏	1998	#4	$1.75
❏	1998	#29 (car)	$1.00
❏	1998	#104	$2.25
❏	1998	Autographs #1	$245.00
❏	1998	Cup Chase #CC5 (car)	$30.00
❏	1998	Oil Cans #OC2 (car)	$10.00
❏	1998	Oil Slicks #4	$4.00
❏	1998	Oil Slicks #29 (car)	$4.00
❏	1998	Pit Stop #PS2 (car)	$12.00
❏	1998	Premium #0	$90.00
❏	1998	Premium #15 (car)	$1.75
❏	1998	Premium #32	$5.00
❏	1998	Premium Flag Chasers #FC20 (car)	$3.75

Press Pass, cont.

			Value
❏	1998	Premium Flag Chasers Reflector #FC20 (car)	$16.00
❏	1998	Premium Reflector #15 (car)	$1.75
❏	1998	Premium Reflector #32	$12.00
❏	1998	Premium Rivalries #R3A	$10.00
❏	1998	Premium Rivalries #R6B (car)	$10.00
❏	1998	Premium Steel Horses #SH2 (car)	$10.00
❏	1998	Premium Triple Gear Fire Suit #TGF2	$350.00
❏	1998	Shockers #ST3A	$22.00
❏	1998	Signings #3	$155.00
❏	1998	Signings Gold #3	$280.00
❏	1998	Stealth #1 (car)	$1.50
❏	1998	Stealth #2 (car)	$1.50
❏	1998	Stealth #59 (car)	$1.50
❏	1998	Stealth Fan Talk #1	$12.00
❏	1998	Stealth Fan Talk Diecut #1	$55.00
❏	1998	Stealth Fusion #1	$4.00
❏	1998	Stealth Fusion #2	$4.00
❏	1998	Stealth Fusion #59 (car)	$4.00
❏	1998	Stealth Octane #OC9 (car)	$3.00
❏	1998	Stealth Octane #OC10 (car)	$3.00
❏	1998	Stealth Octane Diecut #OC9 (car)	N/E
❏	1998	Stealth Octane Diecut #OC10 (car)	N/E
❏	1998	Stealth Race Used Gloves #G8	$285.00
❏	1998	Torpedoes #ST3B (car)	$14.00
❏	1998	Triple Gear "3 in 1" Redemption #STG2	$700.00
❏	1998	Triple Gear Burning Rubber #TG2	$225.00
❏	1998	VIP #6	$3.00
❏	1998	VIP #38 (car)	$1.25
❏	1998	VIP Driving Force #DF5 (car)	$9.00
❏	1998	VIP Driving Force Diecuts #DF5	$16.00
❏	1998	VIP Explosives #6	$4.00
❏	1998	VIP Explosives #38 (car)	$0.75
❏	1998	VIP Head Gear #HG2	$10.00
❏	1998	VIP Head Gear Diecuts #HG2	$20.00
❏	1998	VIP Lap Leader #LL2 (car)	$10.00
❏	1998	VIP Lap Leader Acetate #LL2 (car)	$25.00
❏	1998	VIP NASCAR Country #NC1	$10.00
❏	1998	VIP NASCAR Country Diecuts #NC1	$20.00
❏	1998	VIP Triple Gear "Sheet Metal" #TGS2	$235.00
❏	1999	#8	$2.00
❏	1999	Burning Rubber #BR9	$185.00
❏	1999	Chase Car #SC7B (car)	$13.00
❏	1999	Cup Chase #4	$40.00
❏	1999	Cup Chase #7B	N/E
❏	1999	Oil Cans #3	$9.00
❏	1999	Pit Stop #3	$9.00
❏	1999	Premium #6	$3.00

Page Totals:	How Many	Total Value

Trading Cards

Press Pass, cont.		Value
❏	1999 Premium #35	$1.75
❏	1999 Premium Badge Of Honor #BH19 (car)	$3.00
❏	1999 Premium Badge Of Honor Reflector #BH19 (car)	$19.00
❏	1999 Premium Extreme Fire #FD2A	$40.00
❏	1999 Premium Race Used Fire Suit #F3	$230.00
❏	1999 Premium Reflector #6	$8.00
❏	1999 Premium Reflector #35	$7.00
❏	1999 Premium Steel Horses #SH22 (car)	$9.00
❏	1999 Signings #13	$235.00
❏	1999 Signings Gold #2	N/E
❏	1999 Skidmarks #8	$18.00
❏	1999 Skidmarks #35 (car)	$12.00
❏	1999 Stealth #7	$2.25
❏	1999 Stealth #8 (car)	$0.25
❏	1999 Stealth #53	N/E
❏	1999 Stealth Big Numbers #BN3	$5.00
❏	1999 Stealth Big Numbers Diecut #BN3	N/E
❏	1999 Stealth Fusion #F7	$5.50
❏	1999 Stealth Fusion #F8 (car)	$0.25
❏	1999 Stealth Fusion #F53	$0.25
❏	1999 Stealth Headlines #SH2	$40.00
❏	1999 Stealth Octane SLX #O28 (car)	$0.50
❏	1999 Stealth Octane SLX Diecut #O28 (car)	$0.50
❏	1999 Stealth Race Used Gloves #G3 (car)	$325.00
❏	1999 Stealth SST #SS2 (car)	$12.00
❏	1999 Triple Gear "3 in 1" Redemption #TG9	$680.00
❏	1999 VIP #7	$2.25
❏	1999 VIP #41 (car)	$1.00
❏	1999 VIP Explosives #X7	N/E
❏	1999 VIP Explosives #X41	N/E
❏	1999 VIP Lap Leader #LL3	$12.00
❏	1999 VIP Laser #L7	N/E
❏	1999 VIP Laser #L41 (car)	N/E

Press Pass, cont.		Value
❏	1999 VIP Out Of The Box #OB3 (car)	$3.75
❏	1999 VIP Rear View Mirror #RM3	$4.00
❏	1999 VIP Sheet Metal #SM2 (car)	$170.00
❏	2000 #7	$1.75
❏	2000 Burning Rubber #BR6	$185.00
❏	2000 Burning Rubber Autographs #BR6	N/E
❏	2000 Cup Chase #CC4	$45.00
❏	2000 Gatorade Front Runner	N/E
❏	2000 Millennium #7	$7.00
❏	2000 Oil Cans #OC7 (car)	$4.75
❏	2000 Pit Stop #PS3 (car)	$4.00
❏	2000 Showcar #SC5	N/E
❏	2000 Signings #5	N/E
❏	2000 Signings Gold #3	$275.00
❏	2000 Skidmarks #SK6	$25.00
❏	2000 Techno-Retro #TR6 (car)	$1.00

Pro Set

		Value
❏	1992 #1	$1.75
❏	1992 #59 (car)	$1.00
❏	1992 #161	$1.75
❏	1992 #172 (transporter)	$1.00
❏	1992 #182	$1.75
❏	1992 #224	$1.00
❏	1992 Black #NNO	$80.00
❏	1992 White #NNO	$110.00
❏	1994 Power #2	$1.00
❏	1994 Power #16	$1.00
❏	1994 Power #38	$1.00
❏	1994 Power #59 (transporter)	$0.50
❏	1994 Power Gold Cup #2	$2.25
❏	1994 Power Gold Cup #16	$2.25
❏	1994 Power Gold Cup #38	$2.25
❏	1994 Power Gold Cup #59 (transporter)	$1.00
❏	1994 Power Hologram #NN0	$115.00
❏	1994 Power Preview #31	$1.00

Score Board

		Value
❏	1997 Autographed Racing #1	$1.25
❏	1997 Autographed Racing #36 (car)	$0.65
❏	1997 Autographed Racing #41	$1.50
❏	1997 Autographed Racing #47	$1.00
❏	1997 Autographed Racing #49 (car)	$0.65
❏	1997 Autographed Racing Autographs #12	$200.00
❏	1997 Autographed Racing Mayne Street #KM1	$9.00
❏	1997 I.Q. #1	$3.25
❏	1997 I.Q. #27	$3.25
❏	1997 I.Q. #38	$3.25
❏	1997 I.Q. #40 (car)	$1.50
❏	1997 I.Q. Sam Bass Remarques #SB1	$135.00

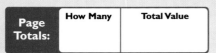

1997 Score Board IQ #1

Page Totals:	How Many	Total Value

1996 Traks Review And Preview #37

Trading Cards

Traks, cont.		Value
1991	Mom-n-Pop's Biscuits #1	$1.75
1991	Mom-n-Pop's Biscuits #2	$1.75
1991	Mom-n-Pop's Biscuits #3	$1.75
1991	Mom-n-Pop's Biscuits #4	$1.75
1991	Mom-n-Pop's Biscuits #5	$1.75
1991	Mom-n-Pop's Biscuits #6	$1.75
1991	Mom-n-Pop's Biscuits (set/6)	$10.00
1991	Mom-n-Pop's Ham #1	$1.75
1991	Mom-n-Pop's Ham #2	$1.75
1991	Mom-n-Pop's Ham #3	$1.75
1991	Mom-n-Pop's Ham #4	$1.75
1991	Mom-n-Pop's Ham #5	$1.75
1991	Mom-n-Pop's Ham #6	$1.75
1991	Mom-n-Pop's Ham (set/6)	$10.00
1991	Richard Petty #22 (car)	$0.50
1992	#3	$1.75
1992	#60	$0.75
1992	#103	$1.25
1992	#175	$0.75
1992	#190	$0.75
1992	#193 (car)	$0.75
1992	Autographs #A1	$180.00
1992	Goody's #19	$2.00
1992	Mom-n-Pop's Ham #1	$3.00
1992	Mom-n-Pop's Ham #2 (car)	$3.00
1992	Mom-n-Pop's Ham #3	$3.00
1992	Mom-n-Pop's Ham #4	$3.00
1992	Mom-n-Pop's Ham #5	$4.00
1992	Mom-n-Pop's Ham #6	$4.00
1992	Mom-n-Pop's Ham (set/6)	$20.00
1992	Mom-n-Pop's Ham Ad w/Coupon	$30.00
1992	Racing Machines #1	$1.00
1992	Racing Machines #3 (car)	$1.00
1992	Racing Machines #9 (car)	$0.75
1992	Racing Machines #34 (car)	$0.75
1992	Racing Machines #44 (car)	$0.75
1992	Racing Machines #54	$0.75
1992	Racing Machines #89	$1.25
1992	Racing Machines #91 (car)	$0.75
1992	Racing Machines #100 (car)	$1.00
1992	Racing Machines Bonus #B3 (car)	$1.00
1992	Team Sets #1 (car)	$0.50
1992	Team Sets #2	$0.75
1992	Team Sets #3 (car)	$0.50
1992	Team Sets #4 (car)	$0.50
1992	Team Sets #13	$0.50
1992	Team Sets #15	$0.50
1992	Team Sets #16 (cars)	$0.75
1992	Team Sets #17	$0.75
1992	Team Sets #18	$0.75
1992	Team Sets #19 (car)	$0.50
1992	Team Sets #20 (car)	$0.50
1992	Team Sets #21	$0.75
1992	Team Sets #22 (airplanes)	$0.50
1992	Team Sets #23	$0.75
1992	Team Sets #24 (cars)	$0.50
1992	Team Sets #25 (car)	$0.50
1992	Team Sets #101 (car)	$0.50

Score Board, cont.		Value
1997	I.Q. Sam Bass Remarques Finished #SB1	N/E
1997	Motorsports #1	$1.25
1997	Motorsports #41	$1.25
1997	Motorsports #47 (car)	$0.75
1997	Motorsports #50 (car)	$0.75
1997	Motorsports #92	$1.25
1997	Motorsports Autographs #AU1	$300.00
1997	Motorsports Race Chat #RC1	$28.00
1997	Motorsports Winston Cup Rewind #WC2 (car)	$5.50

SkyBox

1994	#1	$2.00
1997	Profile #5	$3.00
1997	Profile #63 (car)	$1.50
1997	Profile Autographs #5	$280.00
1997	Profile Pace Setters #E1	$18.00
1997	Profile Team #T4	$120.00

Sports PhotoGraphics

1986	Sports PhotoGraphics #4	$235.00

Traks

1991	#3A	$1.75
1991	#3B	$1.75
1991	#103A	$1.75
1991	#103B	$1.75
1991	#190A	$1.75
1991	#190B	$1.75

Page Totals:	How Many	Total Value

Trading Cards

Traks, cont.		Value
1995	5th Anniversary #3	$1.50
1995	5th Anniversary Clear Contenders #C1	$10.00
1995	5th Anniversary Gold #3	$2.00
1995	5th Anniversary Retrospective #R2	$7.00
1995	5th Anniversary Uncommon Enlarged #E6	$12.00
1995	5th Anniversary Uncommon Enlarged Gold #E6	N/E
1995	#27	$1.25
1995	First Run #27	$3.50
1995	Series Star First Run #SS19	N/E
1996	Review And Preview #37	$1.25
1996	Review And Preview First Run #37	$3.00
1996	Review And Preview Gold #37	N/E
1996	Review And Preview Magnet #37	$15.00

UNO Racing

1983	#27	$62.00

Upper Deck

1996	Road To The Cup #301	$22.00
1996	Road To The Cup #DE1	$55.00
1996	Road To The Cup #RC42	$2.00
1996	Road To The Cup Predictor Points Redemption #PR10	$3.00
1996	SP #3	$3.00
1996	SP Holoview Maximum Effects #ME3	$22.00
1996	SP Holoview Maximum Effects Diecuts #ME3	$165.00
1996	SP #KR1	$110.00
1996	SPx #3	$8.00
1996	SPx Gold #3	$30.00
1997	Collector's Choice #3	$1.00
1997	Collector's Choice 500 #UD1	$1.50
1997	Collector's Choice Victory Circle #VC2	$28.00
1997	Road To The Cup #4	$1.50

1997 Upper Deck Victory Circle Championship Reflections #CR4

Upper Deck, cont.		Value
1997	Road To The Cup #121 (transporter)	$1.00
1997	Road To The Cup Cup Quest #CQ3	$35.00
1997	Road To The Cup Cup Quest Checkered #CQ3	N/E
1997	Road To The Cup Cup Quest White #CQ3	N/E
1997	Road To The Cup Premier Position #PP4	$7.00
1997	SP #3	$28.00
1997	SP #45 (car)	$13.00
1997	SP Race Film #RD3	$135.00
1997	SP Super Series #3	$80.00
1997	SP Super Series #45 (car)	$75.00
1997	SPx #3	$4.00
1997	SPx Blue #3	$3.00
1997	SPx Gold #3	$70.00
1997	SPx Silver #3	$5.50
1997	Victory Circle #3	$1.50
1997	Victory Circle Championship Reflections #CR4	$6.50
1997	Victory Circle Driver's Seat #DS1	$48.00
1997	Victory Circle Victory Lap #VL1	$110.00
1998	Collector's Choice #3	$1.25
1998	Collector's Choice #39 (car)	$0.35
1998	Collector's Choice #103	$0.50
1998	Collector's Choice Star Quest #SQ26	$10.00
1998	Diamond Vision #3	$13.00
1998	Diamond Vision Signature Moves #3	N/E
1998	Diamond Vision Vision Of A Champion #VC2	$70.00
1998	Road To The Cup #3	$3.00
1998	Road To The Cup #75	$3.00
1998	Road To The Cup 50th Anniversary #AN49	$7.00
1998	Road To The Cup 50th Anniversary Autographs #AN49	$325.00
1998	Road To The Cup Cover Story #CS10	$7.25
1998	SP Authentic #3	$3.00
1998	SP Authentic #37 (car)	$1.50
1998	SP Authentic Sign Of The Times Level 2 #ST3	$210.00
1998	SP Authentic Traditions #T1	$350.00
1998	Victory Circle #3	$3.50
1998	Victory Circle #48 (car)	$1.50
1998	Victory Circle Point Leaders #PL5	$20.00
1998	Victory Circle Sparks Of Brilliance #SB3	$75.00
1999	Road To The Cup #26	$2.00
1999	Road To The Cup #60 (car)	$0.25
1999	Road To The Cup	

Page Totals:	How Many	Total Value

1996 Wheels Knight Quest #22

Upper Deck, cont.

	Value
2000 Victory Circle #9	N/E
2000 Victory Circle #55 (car)	N/E
2000 Victory Circle #70 (car)	N/E
2000 Victory Circle Exclusives Level 1 #9	N/E
2000 Victory Circle Exclusives Level 1 #55	N/E
2000 Victory Circle Exclusives Level 1 #70	N/E
2000 Victory Circle Exclusives Level 2 #9	N/E
2000 Victory Circle Exclusives Level 2 #55	N/E
2000 Victory Circle Exclusives Level 2 #70	N/E
2000 Victory Circle PowerDeck #PD1	$16.00
2000 Victory Circle Winning Material Tire #TDE	N/E

Wheels

	Value
1992 Special Tribute Gold #1	$2.50
1992 Special Tribute Gold Autographs #1	$5.00
1992 Special Tribute Platinum #1	$2.50
1992 Special Tribute Silver #1	$2.50
1993 Mom-n-Pop's #1	$1.75
1993 Mom-n-Pop's #2	$1.75
1993 Mom-n-Pop's #3	$1.75
1993 Mom-n-Pop's #4	$1.75
1993 Mom-n-Pop's #5	$1.75
1993 Mom-n-Pop's #6	$1.75
1993 Mom-n-Pop's (set/6)	$10.00
1994 High Gear #1	$1.75
1994 High Gear #79	$0.75
1994 High Gear #85	$0.75
1994 High Gear #92	$0.75
1994 High Gear #186	$0.75
1994 High Gear #188	$0.75
1994 High Gear Day One #186	$0.75
1994 High Gear Day One #188	$0.75
1994 High Gear Day One Gold #186	$2.50
1994 High Gear Day One Gold #188	$2.50
1994 High Gear Dominators #D3	$35.00
1994 High Gear Gold #1	$15.00
1994 High Gear Gold #188	$5.00
1994 High Gear Mega Gold #MG1	$3.50
1994 High Gear Mega Gold #SMG1	$45.00
1994 High Gear Power Pack Teams #E3	$2.25
1994 High Gear Power Pack Teams #E4	$2.25
1994 High Gear Power Pack Teams #E5	$2.25
1994 High Gear Power Pack Teams #E18	$0.75
1994 High Gear Power Pack	

Upper Deck, cont.

	Value
Motorsports #NC11	$4.75
1999 Road To The Cup NASCAR Chronicles #NC11	$5.00
1999 Road To The Cup Upper Deck Profiles #P3	$12.00
1999 SP Authentic #2	$3.00
1999 SP Authentic #53 (car)	$25.00
1999 SP Authentic #79	$20.00
1999 SP Authentic Driving Force #DF7	$9.00
1999 SP Authentic In The Driver's Seat #DS1	$5.00
1999 SP Authentic Overdrive #79	N/E
1999 SP Authentic Sign Of The Times #7	$210.00
1999 Victory Circle #26	$2.00
1999 Victory Circle #60	N/E
1999 Victory Circle #83	$2.00
1999 Victory Circle NASCAR Signature Collection #DE	$18.00
1999 Victory Circle Victory Circle #V1	$15.00
2000 MVP #3	$2.00
2000 MVP #87 (car)	$1.00
2000 MVP Cup Quest #3	$3.00
2000 MVP Cup Quest #CQ1	N/E
2000 MVP Gold Script #3	$30.00
2000 MVP Gold Script #87	N/E
2000 MVP NASCAR Stars #NS3	$3.00
2000 MVP SIlver Script #3	N/E
2000 MVP SIlver Script #87	N/E
2000 MVP Super Script #3	N/E

Page Totals:	How Many	Total Value

Trading Cards

		Wheels, cont.	Value
❏		Teams #E19	$0.75
❏	1994	High Gear Power Pack Teams #E20 (car)	$2.25
❏	1994	High Gear Power Pack Teams #E21 (car)	$1.25
❏	1994	High Gear Rookie Update #104	$5.00
❏	1994	High Gear Rookie Update Platinum #104	$12.00
❏	1995	Crown Jewels #1	$2.25
❏	1995	Crown Jewels #64 (car)	$0.65
❏	1995	Crown Jewels Diamond #1	$84.00
❏	1995	Crown Jewels Diamond #64 (car)	$20.00
❏	1995	Crown Jewels Dual Jewels #DJ1	$35.00
❏	1995	Crown Jewels Dual Jewels #DJ6	$30.00
❏	1995	Crown Jewels Emerald #1	$38.00
❏	1995	Crown Jewels Emerald #64 (car)	$10.00
❏	1995	Crown Jewels Signature Gems #SG3	$26.00
❏	1995	High Gear #1	$1.75
❏	1995	High Gear #71 (car)	$1.75
❏	1995	High Gear #86	$1.00
❏	1995	High Gear Busch Clash #BC8	$3.00
❏	1995	High Gear Busch Clash Gold #BC8	$28.00
❏	1995	High Gear Day One #1	$3.00
❏	1995	High Gear Day One #71 (car)	$1.00
❏	1995	High Gear Day One #86	$1.75
❏	1995	High Gear Day One Gold #1	$6.00
❏	1995	High Gear Day One Gold #71 (car)	$4.00
❏	1995	High Gear Day One Gold #86	$5.00
❏	1995	High Gear Dominators #D3	$18.00
❏	1995	High Gear Gold #1	$6.00
❏	1995	High Gear Gold #71	$3.00
❏	1995	High Gear Gold #86	$3.00
❏	1995	High Gear Mini-Dominators #MD3	$18.00
❏	1996	Crown Jewels #1	$1.75

1996 Wheels Viper Diamondback #D2

		Wheels, cont.	Value
❏	1996	Crown Jewels Elite #1	$1.75
❏	1996	Crown Jewels Elite #27	$1.75
❏	1996	Crown Jewels Elite #56	$0.75
❏	1996	Crown Jewels Elite #57 (transporter)	$0.75
❏	1996	Crown Jewels Elite 7 Gems	$90.00
❏	1996	Crown Jewels Elite 7 Gems Diamonds	$220.00
❏	1996	Crown Jewels Elite 7 Gems Treasure Chest	$125.00
❏	1996	Crown Jewels Elite Birthstones Of The Champions #BC1	$85.00
❏	1996	Crown Jewels Elite Birthstones Of The Champions Treasure Chest #BC1	N/E
❏	1996	Crown Jewels Elite Diamond Tribute Crown Signature Amethyst #CS1	$22.00
❏	1996	Crown Jewels Elite Dual Jewels Amethyst #DJ1	$30.00
❏	1996	Crown Jewels Elite Dual Jewels Amethyst Tresure Chest #DJ1	N/E
❏	1996	Crown Jewels Elite Dual Jewels Garnet #DJ1	$20.00
❏	1996	Crown Jewels Elite Dual Jewels Garnet Treasure Chest #DJ1	N/E
❏	1996	Crown Jewels Elite Dual Jewels Sapphire #DJ1	$60.00
❏	1996	Crown Jewels Elite Dual Jewels Sapphire Treasure Chest #DJ1	N/E
❏	1996	Crown Jewels Elite Emerald #1	$20.00
❏	1996	Crown Jewels Elite Emerald #27	$20.00
❏	1996	Crown Jewels Elite Emerald #56	$8.00
❏	1996	Crown Jewels Elite Emerald #57 (transporter)	$8.00
❏	1996	Crown Jewels Elite Emerald Treasure Chest #1	$26.00
❏	1996	Crown Jewels Elite Emerald Treasure Chest #27	$26.00
❏	1996	Crown Jewels Elite Emerald Treasure Chest #56	$12.00
❏	1996	Crown Jewels Elite Emerald Treasure Chest #57 (transporter)	$12.00
❏	1996	Crown Jewels Elite Sapphire #1	$8.00
❏	1996	Crown Jewels Elite Sapphire #27	$8.00
❏	1996	Crown Jewels Elite Sapphire #56	$5.00
❏	1996	Crown Jewels Elite Sapphire #57 (transporter)	$5.00
❏	1996	KnightQuest #1	$1.75
❏	1996	KnightQuest #22	$1.75
❏	1996	KnightQuest #25	$1.75

Page Totals:	How Many	Total Value

1998 Wheels 50th Anniversary #A18

	Wheels, cont.	Value
❑	1996 Viper Black Mamba #43	$35.00
❑	1996 Viper Black Mamba #R3	$85.00
❑	1996 Viper Busch Clash #B14	$20.00
❑	1996 Viper Cobra #C1	$32.00
❑	1996 Viper Cobra First Strike #C1	$80.00
❑	1996 Viper Copperhead #1	$15.00
❑	1996 Viper Copperhead #43	$15.00
❑	1996 Viper Copperhead First Strike #1	$25.00
❑	1996 Viper Copperhead First Strike #43	$25.00
❑	1996 Viper Diamondback #D2	$55.00
❑	1996 Viper Diamondback Authentic #DA2	$135.00
❑	1996 Viper Diamondback Authentic California #DB2	N/E
❑	1996 Viper Diamondback Authentic First Strike #DA2	N/E
❑	1996 Viper Diamondback First Strike #D2	N/E
❑	1996 Viper First Strike #1	$4.00
❑	1996 Viper First Strike #43	$4.00
❑	1996 Viper Green Mamba #1	$55.00
❑	1996 Viper Green Mamba #43	$55.00
❑	1996 Viper Green Mamba #R3	$85.00
❑	1996 Viper King Cobra #KC1	$50.00
❑	1996 Viper King Cobra First Strike KC1	N/E
❑	1996 Viper Mom-n-Pop's #1	$10.00
❑	1996 Viper Mom-n-Pop's #2	$10.00
❑	1996 Viper Mom-n-Pop's #3	$10.00
❑	1996 Viper Red Cobra #1	$3.00
❑	1996 Viper Red Cobra #43	$3.00
❑	1996 Viper Venom Dale Earnhardt #1	$20.00
❑	1996 Viper Venom Dale Earnhardt #2	$20.00
❑	1996 Viper Venom Dale Earnhardt #3	$20.00
❑	1996 Viper Venom Dale Earnhardt (set/3)	$65.00
❑	1997 Jurassic Park Carnivore #C1	$24.00
❑	1997 Jurassic Park Pteranodon #P1	$33.00
❑	1997 Jurassic Park T-Rex #TR5	$60.00
❑	1997 Predator #3	$2.00
❑	1997 Predator American Eagle #AE1	$22.00
❑	1997 Predator American Eagle First Slash #AE1	N/E
❑	1997 Predator Black Wolf First Strike #3	$0.75
❑	1997 Predator Eye Of The Tiger #ET1	$13.00
❑	1997 Predator Eye Of The Tiger First Slash #ET1	$45.00
❑	1997 Predator First Slash #3	$4.00
❑	1997 Predator Gatorback #GB1	$33.00
❑	1997 Predator Gatorback Authentic #GBA1	N/E

	Wheels, cont.	Value
❑	1996 KnightQuest Black Knights #1	$26.00
❑	1996 KnightQuest Black Knights #22	$26.00
❑	1996 KnightQuest Black Knights #25	$26.00
❑	1996 KnightQuest First Knights #FK1	$26.00
❑	1996 KnightQuest Knights Of The Round Table #KT1	$50.00
❑	1996 KnightQuest Protectors Of The Crown #PC2	$80.00
❑	1996 KnightQuest Red Knight Preview #1	$3.00
❑	1996 KnightQuest Red Knight Preview #22	$3.00
❑	1996 KnightQuest Red Knight Preview #25	$3.00
❑	1996 KnightQuest Santa Claus #SC1	$40.00
❑	1996 KnightQuest White Knights #1	$26.00
❑	1996 KnightQuest White Knights #22	$26.00
❑	1996 KnightQuest White Knights #25	$26.00
❑	1996 Mom-n-Pop's #MPC1	$4.00
❑	1996 Mom-n-Pop's #MPC2	$4.00
❑	1996 Mom-n-Pop's #MPC3	$4.00
❑	1996 Mom-n-Pop's MPC (set/3)	$13.00
❑	1996 Viper #1	$2.00
❑	1996 Viper #43	$1.50
❑	1996 Viper Black Mamba #1	$35.00

Trading Cards

Wheels, cont.	Value
1997 Predator Gatorback Authentic First Slash #GBA1	N/E
1997 Predator Gatorback First Slash #GB1	N/E
1997 Predator Golden Eagle #GE1	$33.00
1997 Predator Grizzly #3	$12.00
1997 Predator Grizzly First Slash #3	$18.00
1997 Predator Red Wolf #3	N/E
1997 Predator Red Wolf First Slash #3	N/E
1997 Race Sharks #1	$2.00
1997 Race Sharks First Bite #1	$3.00
1997 Race Sharks First Bite Shark Attack #SA1	$575.00
1997 Race Sharks First Bite Shark Attack Preview #3	$18.00
1997 Race Sharks Great White #GW1	$90.00
1997 Race Sharks Great White First Bite #GW1	N/E
1997 Race Sharks Great White Parallel #1	N/E
1997 Race Sharks Hammerhead #1	$15.00
1997 Race Sharks Hammerhead First Bite # 1	N/E
1997 Race Sharks Shark Attack #SA1	$30.00
1997 Race Sharks Shark Tooth Signature #ST1	$180.00
1997 Race Sharks Shark Tooth Signature First Bite #ST1	N/E
1997 Race Sharks Tiger Shark #1	$18.00
1997 Race Sharks Tiger Shark First Bite #1	$25.00
1997 Viper #68 (car)	$2.50
1997 Viper Anaconda #A5	$35.00
1997 Viper Black Racer #68 (car)	$7.00
1997 Viper Black Racer First Strike #68 (car)	$7.00
1997 Viper Cobra #C1	$20.00
1997 Viper Cobra First Strike #C1	$300.00

1996 Wheels Crown Jewels Elite #56

Wheels, cont.	Value
1997 Viper Diamondback #DB8	$45.00
1997 Viper Diamondback Authentic Eastern #DBA8	$100.00
1997 Viper Diamondback Authentic Eastern First Strike #DBA8	N/E
1997 Viper Diamondback Authentic Western #DBA8	$100.00
1997 Viper Diamondback Authentic Western First Strike #DBA8	$100.00
1997 Viper Diamondback First Strike #DB8	N/E
1997 Viper First Strike #68 (car)	$1.25
1997 Viper King Cobra #KC1	$45.00
1997 Viper Snake Eyes #SE1	$18.00
1997 Viper Snake Eyes First Strike #SE1	$175.00
1998 50th Anniversary #A3	$6.00
1998 50th Anniversary #A18 (car)	$2.00
1998 #9	$2.00
1998 #34 (car)	$1.00
1998 #83	$2.00
1998 #99 (car)	$1.00
1998 Autographs #1	$185.00
1998 Double Take #E2	$55.00
1998 Golden #9	N/E
1998 Golden #34 (car)	N/E
1998 Golden #83	N/E
1998 Golden #99 (car)	N/E
1998 Green Flags #GF4 (car)	$10.00
1998 High Gear #5	$2.25
1998 High Gear #29 (car)	$0.50
1998 High Gear #48 (car)	$0.50
1998 High Gear #64 (car)	$0.75
1998 High Gear Autographs #6	$310.00
1998 High Gear Custom Shop Redemption #CS1	$150.00
1998 High Gear First Gear #5	N/E
1998 High Gear First Gear #29 (car)	N/E
1998 High Gear First Gear #48 (car)	N/E
1998 High Gear First Gear #64 (car)	N/E
1998 High Gear Gear Jammers #GJ2 (car)	$3.00
1998 High Gear High Groove #HG2 (car)	$7.00
1998 High Gear Man And Machine #MM7A	$17.00
1998 High Gear Man And Machine #MM7B (car)	$12.00
1998 High Gear MPH #5	$50.00
1998 High Gear MPH #29 (car)	$25.00
1998 High Gear MPH #48 (car)	$25.00
1998 High Gear MPH #64 (car)	$25.00
1998 High Gear Pure Gold #PG1	$6.50
1998 High Gear Top Tier #TT5	$10.00
1998 Jackpot #J1	$10.00
1999 #9	$2.00
1999 #56 (car)	$0.25
1999 Circuit Breaker #CB3	$15.00
1999 Dialed In #DI3 (car)	$4.75

Page Totals: How Many / Total Value

Collector's Value Guide™ – Dale Earnhardt®

1997 Wheels Predator #3

Wheels, cont.			Value
❏	1999	Flag Chasers Daytona 7 Black #DS2	$195.00
❏	1999	Flag Chasers Daytona 7 Blue-Yellow #DS2	$330.00
❏	1999	Flag Chasers Daytona 7 Checkered #DS2	$390.00
❏	1999	Flag Chasers Daytona 7 Green #DS2	$185.00
❏	1999	Flag Chasers Daytona 7 Red #DS2	$185.00
❏	1999	Flag Chasers Daytona 7 White #DS2	$185.00
❏	1999	Flag Chasers Daytona 7 Yellow #DS2	N/E
❏	1999	Golden #9	$75.00
❏	1999	Golden #56 (car)	$3.00
❏	1999	High Gear #8	$2.25
❏	1999	High Gear #29 (car)	$1.00
❏	1999	High Gear #48 (car)	$1.00
❏	1999	High Gear #64 (car)	$1.00
❏	1999	High Gear Authentic Signature	N/E
❏	1999	High Gear Autographs #6	$240.00
❏	1999	High Gear Custom Shop Redemption #CSDE	$60.00
❏	1999	High Gear First Gear #8	N/E
❏	1999	High Gear First Gear #29	N/E
❏	1999	High Gear First Gear #37	N/E
❏	1999	High Gear First Gear #48	N/E
❏	1999	High Gear First Gear #64	N/E
❏	1999	High Gear Flag Chasers Black #FC5 (car)	$200.00

Wheels, cont.			Value
❏	1999	High Gear Flag Chasers Blue-Yellow #FC5 (car)	$340.00
❏	1999	High Gear Flag Chasers Checkered #FC5 (car)	$300.00
❏	1999	High Gear Flag Chasers Green #FC5 (car)	$250.00
❏	1999	High Gear Flag Chasers Red #FC5 (car)	$250.00
❏	1999	High Gear Flag Chasers White #FC5 (car)	$200.00
❏	1999	High Gear Flag Chasers Yellow #FC5 (car)	$200.00
❏	1999	High Gear Gear Shifters #GS8	$4.75
❏	1999	High Gear Hot Streaks #HS3 (car)	$3.00
❏	1999	High Gear MPH #8	N/E
❏	1999	High Gear MPH #29 (car)	$4.00
❏	1999	High Gear MPH #48 (car)	$4.00
❏	1999	High Gear MPH #64 (car)	$4.00
❏	1999	High Gear Sunday Sensation #SS7	N/E
❏	1999	High Gear Top Tier #TT8 (car)	$4.75
❏	1999	High Gear Winning Edge #WE6	N/E
❏	1999	High Groove #HG4 (car)	$4.00
❏	1999	Runnin And Gunnin #RG3 (car)	$2.50
❏	1999	Runnin And Gunnin Foil Etched #RG3 (car)	$10.00
❏	2000	High Gear #7	N/E
❏	2000	High Gear Autographs #9	
❏	2000	High Gear First Gear #7	N/E
❏	2000	High Gear Flag Chasers #FC3	N/E
❏	2000	High Gear Gear Shifters #GS7	N/E
❏	2000	High Gear MPH #7	N/E
❏	2000	High Gear Top Tier #TT7	N/E
❏	2000	High Gear Winning Edge #WE6	N/E

WSMP

❏	1995	The Next Generation #1	$5.00
❏	1995	The Next Generation #2	$5.00
❏	1995	The Next Generation #3	$5.00
❏	1995	The Next Generation #NNO	$5.00

Page Totals:	How Many	Total Value

Future Releases

Check our web site, *CollectorsQuest.com*, for new
Dale Earnhardt product releases and record the information here.

Future Releases

Die-Cast Cars	Value	How Many	Total Value

Page Totals:	How Many	Total Value

COLLECTOR'S
VALUE GUIDE™

148

Future Releases

Check our web site, *CollectorsQuest.com*, for new
Dale Earnhardt product releases and record the information here.

Other Collectibles	Value	How Many	Total Value
Trading Cards			

	How Many	Total Value
Page Totals:		

Total Value Of My Collection

Record your collection here by adding the totals from
the bottom of each Value Guide page.

Total Value Of My Collection

Die-Cast Cars			Die-Cast Cars		
Page #	How Many	Total Value	Page #	How Many	Total Value
Page 37			Page 56		
Page 38			Page 57		
Page 39			Page 58		
Page 40			Page 59		
Page 41			Page 60		
Page 42			Page 61		
Page 43			Page 62		
Page 44			Page 63		
Page 45			Page 64		
Page 46			Page 65		
Page 47			Page 66		
Page 48			Page 67		
Page 49			Page 68		
Page 50			Page 69		
Page 51			Page 70		
Page 52			Page 71		
Page 53			Page 72		
Page 54			Page 73		
Page 55			Page 74		
Subtotal			**Subtotal**		

Page Totals:	How Many	Total Value

COLLECTOR'S
VALUE GUIDE™

150

Total Value Of My Collection

Record your collection here by adding the totals from
the bottom of each Value Guide page.

Die-Cast Cars				Other Collectibles		
Page #	How Many	Total Value		Page #	How Many	Total Value
Page 75				Page 93		
Page 76				Page 94		
Page 77				Page 95		
Page 78				Page 96		
Page 79				Page 97		
Page 80				Page 98		
Page 81				Page 99		
Page 82				Page 100		
Page 83				Page 101		
Page 84				Page 102		
Page 85				Page 103		
Page 86				Page 104		
Page 87				Page 105		
Page 88				Page 106		
Page 89				Page 107		
Page 90				Page 108		
Page 91				Page 109		
Page 92				Page 110		
Subtotal				**Subtotal**		

COLLECTOR'S
VALUE GUIDE™

Page Totals:	How Many	Total Value

Total Value Of My Collection

Record your collection here by adding the totals from
the bottom of each Value Guide page.

Other Collectibles

Page #	How Many	Total Value
Page 111		
Page 112		
Page 113		
Page 114		
Page 115		
Page 116		
Page 117		
Page 118		
Page 119		
Page 120		
Page 121		
Page 122		
Page 123		
Page 124		
Page 125		

Trading Cards

Page #	How Many	Total Value
Page 126		
Page 127		
Page 128		
Subtotal		

Trading Cards

Page #	How Many	Total Value
Page 129		
Page 130		
Page 131		
Page 132		
Page 133		
Page 134		
Page 135		
Page 136		
Page 137		
Page 138		
Page 139		
Page 140		
Page 141		
Page 142		
Page 143		
Page 144		
Page 145		
Page 146		
Page 147		
Subtotal		

Page Totals:	How Many	Total Value

COLLECTOR'S
VALUE GUIDE™

Other Products & Accessories

As loyal fans know, the world of Dale Earnhardt collectibles doesn't stop at die-cast cars and collector trading cards – not by a long shot! There are a host of other products and accessory items that feature photographs of Earnhardt or one of his race cars, his signature or his team colors.

For the fashion conscious, there are all sorts of apparel and accessory items to choose from, including Earnhardt hats, T-shirts, sweatshirts and belt buckles. There are replica racing uniforms and helmets that are both unique collector's items and fun ways to show your support of your favorite driver.

Fans can turn a study or bedroom into an "Earnhardt Room" with a selection of "Intimidator"-themed home accessories, such as pillows, chairs, wallpaper, clocks or ceiling fans. Or you can add some racing excitement to your Christmas tree with an Earnhardt ornament, or keep the memory of Earnhardt in your kitchen all year-round with collector plates, coffee mugs and shot glasses.

For kids and kids-at-heart alike, there are a variety of Earnhardt games and toys, including board games, computer games, electronic games, plush toys, model cars and radio-controlled cars. Sports enthusiasts will enjoy such Earnhardt products as golf accessories and hunting knives, while collectors of the more nostalgic and unique items might want to track down Earnhardt-themed soda bottles, lighters, cereal boxes and telephone cards. With so many collectible and functional items to choose from, a determined Earnhardt collector could keep busy collecting for a long time!

Other Products & Accessories

Remote-Controlled & Model Cars
Some Assembly Required

Anyone who has ever wanted to be on Dale Earnhardt's pit crew might enjoy putting together one of his race cars at home. Many of his cars have been produced as model replicas, such as the ProFinish™ Snaptite version of Earnhardt's 1998 Goodwrench Plus car.

His cars have also been recreated as radio-controlled versions, including a 1:12 scale of the 2000 Goodwrench Plus car that speeds along at 20 mph.

Phone Cards
Collect From Kannapolis

Collectible phone cards have been randomly distributed inside packs of NASCAR trading cards since 1995, and since then have been popular with Dale Earnhardt collectors.

The first calling card that featured "The Intimidator" was manufactured by Assets and contained $1 worth of phone time. Since then, Earnhardt calling cards have been produced in amounts that range from $1 to $1,000. Some phone cards feature several NASCAR drivers (including Earnhardt) and are extremely rare.

Cereal Boxes
Breakfast Of 7-Time Champions

In 1997, Dale Earnhardt appeared on four different Wheaties® boxes: two regular boxes, one with a photograph of Earnhardt on the front and another with a drawing of Earnhardt and his car; a Honey Frosted Wheaties® box, featuring Earnhardt in his Wheaties fire suit with his Wheaties car; and a Crispy Wheaties 'n Raisins® box, showing Earnhardt posed in an intimidating, crossed-arms position beside his Wheaties car. All four boxes feature Earnhardt's signature on the front.

The Kellogg Company, one of the most recognizable names in breakfast foods, released five Earnhardt cereal boxes in the 1990s. The company issued two Kellogg's® Corn Flakes® boxes, one each in 1994 and 1995, to commemorate "The Intimidator's" sixth and seventh Winston Cup Championships. In 1996, Earnhardt was featured on a Kellogg's® Frosted Flakes® box. Finally, Earnhardt also appeared on two Kellogg's® Frosted Mini-Wheats® boxes; one, issued in 1995, showed Earnhardt with Jeff Gordon under the title "The Kid and the Champ;" the second, released in 1997, featured Earnhardt by himself.

Action Figures
Pint-Sized Intimidation

Dale Earnhardt fans and collectors alike can thank Kenner® (now a division of Hasbro Inc.) for the 26 action figures of "The Intimidator" at various points in his career. Introduced in 1997, these action figures are part of the Winner's Circle® collection, and some have been produced exclusively for selected retail outlets. Eight figures are to be released throughout the year 2000 in honor of Earnhardt's most illustrious wins. Each figure stands 5" tall and comes with a collectible card.

Lighters
Internal Combustion

Since the 1930s, Zippo Manufacturing Company has produced quality weatherproof lighters in hundreds of designs. Recently, those designs have included commemorative NASCAR racing lighters.

Collectors can find lighters that feature Dale Earnhardt's likeness, the stylized #3 and his Monte Carlo. Fans can even celebrate his 1995 speed record with a limited edition Brickyard 400 lighter.

Immensely popular with smokers and non-smokers alike, these Earnhardt lighters are sure to "fire up" any collection.

Helmets
Keep It Under Your Hat

Although he has nerves to spare, even Dale Earnhardt recognizes the need for a strong helmet out on the tracks. Now dedicated fans can own replicas of Earnhardt's distinctive headgear.

The Racing Collectables Club of America has replicated nearly all of Earnhardt's Winston Select racing car paint schemes on 1:4-scale helmets. These authentic representations of the Simpson® helmets worn by Earnhardt are numbered limited editions and come with certificates of authenticity.

Collector Plates
Dish It Out

A number of collector plates have been issued in honor of Dale Earnhardt and the milestones of his illustrious career. One of the better known plate manufacturers, The Hamilton Collection has issued a variety of Earnhardt-themed designs since 1995. The 6-1/2"-diameter limited edition plates are hand numbered, bordered in 24K gold and come with certificates of authenticity. Most plates display pictures of Earnhardt with his car.

Collector Knives
On The Cutting Edge

Knives can be more than just weapons or tools. Exquisite craftsmanship and artistic design can make a knife a sought-after collectible. Dale Earnhardt's passion for hunting and the outdoor life has inspired a line of signature knives collectors will be proud to display in their homes.

Over the years, Frost Cutlery and Case Knives have produced many different types of commemorative Earnhardt knives. For example, the Earnhardt Bowie knife is a foot-long work of art graced with Earnhardt's image and car on the blade, and his signature on the handle.

If your collectibles shelf doesn't have space for a large knife, you can also find 4" lock-back knives with nickel and silver blades. Some of these knives come with engraved ivory handles or handles shaped to resemble Earnhardt's Monte Carlo.

Of course, knives can be functional as well as decorative. The 3" Earnhardt knives are perfect for emergencies. And there's even an Earnhardt pocket knife, complete with saw, scissors, screwdriver and other blades for just about every need and occasion.

Clothing
The Fashionable Dale Earnhardt®

Fans of the legendary "Man In Black" can profess their loyalty with clothing for nearly all occasions. After all, a driver whose first big sponsor was a jeans company is bound to have a stylish side! NASCAR's official trackside outfitter, Chase Authentics, is just one of the many companies producing Dale Earnhardt apparel of the highest quality.

There's no better way to show your support for "The Intimidator" than with a stylish T-shirt. Many have been spotted for the Goodwrench and Wrangler cars, and the Peter Max car made an appearance as the first #3 tie-dyed shirt. And if the weather at the racetrack is unfavorable, you can keep warm with an Earnhardt sweatshirt, jacket or hat.

A die-hard Earnhardt fan can even purchase a reproduction of Earnhardt's racing uniform. And for Earnhardt's youngest fans, there are #3 infant sleepers and baby shoes.

With Earnhardt apparel for all ages and personal tastes, all fans can look their best both at the track and at home.

One T-Shirt Says . . .

"You Don't Just Get It . . .
You Have to EARN IT."

Glassware
Drinking With Dale Earnhardt

Dale Earnhardt's NASCAR sponsors have included soft drink and beer companies, so it's no surprise that his likeness can be found on glassware items. There's a variety of choices, from a lug nut-shaped coffee mug to make that morning caffeine rush all the better, to a lug nut-shaped shot glass. If you're a beer drinker or a stein collector, one of the steins featuring Earnhardt's image and number may be just the thing to make your collection complete. And you won't want to go to the track without your #3 bottle opener, or a water bottle shaped like the pit crew's gas can!

Watches & Clocks
Time To Race!

Need to be on time for a race? Dale Earnhardt Inc. has licensed a number of wristwatches and pocket watches that feature images of Dale Earnhardt, his car and the stylized #3. If you'd rather have a wall clock, check out the timepieces by JEBCO Clocks Inc. One series pays tribute to Earnhardt's career and his accomplishments, including his seven Winston Cup Championships, while another series features original artwork by such artists as Sam Bass.

Soda
A Thirst For Speed

Stock car driving is thirsty work. So, soft drink companies have been involved with NASCAR drivers for years, and Dale Earnhardt is no exception. Beverage merchandising with his name includes one of the most recognized names in the world of soda and one of the more obscure.

As the first official soft drink sponsor of NASCAR, the Coca-Cola Company was a natural choice to produce a line of Dale Earnhardt collectibles. Coca-Cola introduced the "Coca-Cola® Racing Family," featuring four of NASCAR's best drivers. Earnhardt is pictured on one of these bottles with his #3 on the label and the bottle cap.

But Coke wasn't the only soft drink to honor "The Intimidator." He has also been on bottles of Sun-drop™ citrus soda made by Dr. Pepper/Seven Up Inc., which is popular in the southeastern United States. To celebrate Earnhardt's success on the track, the company produced six commemorative bottles bearing his image. Each one honors one of Earnhardt's achievements: one for his Rookie of the Year title in 1979 and five others for his first five Winston Cup Championships.

The 1986 Sun-drop bottle pictures a small insert of Earnhardt leaping into the air. The 1987 bottle pictures his car ahead of several others. Earnhardt's #3 car is featured solo on the 1990 bottle, and in 1991, Earnhardt is pictured holding the Championship Cup.

Ornaments
Driving Around The Christmas Tree

When Christmas rolls around, Dale Earnhardt collectors can deck their Christmas trees with a handsome collection of ornaments that celebrate "The Intimidator's" outstanding career.

Hallmark Cards Inc. issued a special ornament honoring Earnhardt in 2000. And the Racing Collectables Club of America™ has issued two limited edition gold-plated ornaments. Collectors who prefer more simple or traditional designs can choose from any number of ball ornaments, bearing Earnhardt's likeness. But watch out – your Earnhardt ornaments might want to race your other decorations to the top of the tree!

Golf Items
A Different Kind Of Driver

Stock car driving is certainly Dale Earnhardt's sport of choice. But many of his loyal fans might practice a different sport – the game of golf. Products from Sports Image Inc. and Sun Time Enterprises let you "intimidate" your opponents on the links.

On the course, you can bring along an assortment of Earnhardt-themed golf items in a golf bag from Sports Image Inc., club head covers, golf balls, driver and putter. And die-hard fans can even repair damaged turf with an Earnhardt divot tool!

Games
Playing With The Pro!

Looking to expand your collection? Parker Brothers' popular board game *Monopoly*® now comes in a collector's edition customized with a Dale Earnhardt theme. Instead of "Community Chest" and "Chance" cards, the game includes "Green Flag" and "Checkered Flag" cards. Players can race around the board with such tokens as a winner's trophy or a pit crewman. The object: to gain ownership of the race cars Earnhardt has driven during his career.

Checkered Flag
BLACK FLAG
GO DIRECTLY TO JAIL
DO NOT PASS GO, DO NOT COLLECT $200

Another board game featuring Earnhardt is *NASCAR Champions*, which has "The Intimidator" racing against other NASCAR greats for the biggest purse. This Milton Bradley game also includes collectible driver cards.

Green Flag
PIT CREW CHAMPIONS
YOU GET $45

Various video games pay tribute to both NASCAR and Earnhardt, including *NASCAR Racer* (an electronic key chain game) and *NASCAR Pacesetter* (a car with a pop-up video game in the trunk). Older fans can enjoy a host of NASCAR games for Playstation®, Nintendo™ or home personal computers. The *NASCAR Heat* video game was slated to debut for the 2000 holiday season. Earnhardt fans will think they're behind the wheel of the #3 Monte Carlo!

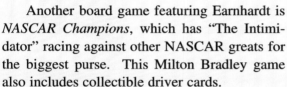

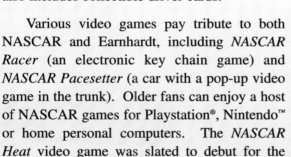

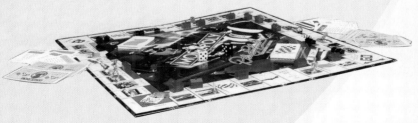

COLLECTOR'S
VALUE GUIDE™

Dale Earnhardt® Products & Accessories

Plush
Hugging The Turns

Squeezable cars and #3 teddy bears – no Dale Earnhardt collection is complete without them!

Plush and bean bag collectibles, particularly sports-related items, have been the rage for years. Team Beans™, a well-known name in sports plush toys, has introduced the Speed Beans™ line that consists of several different NASCAR bears. They include a bear decked out in a replica of Earnhardt's uniform, a series of bears honoring the last five winners of the Brickyard 400 and many other cuddly creations.

Celebrity Bears, a division of JC Bears Inc., commemorates celebrities from Hollywood to Washington with a series of plush bruins. The black and white "Dale Earnhardt Sr. Celebrity Bear #59" features a red race car on its chest and wears a #3 black and white checkered hat.

Also, collectors can purchase bean bag replicas of stock cars produced by various manufacturers. These soft keepsakes will make any Earnhardt collection huggable!

Secondary Market Overview

Dale Earnhardt's years of successful racing have propelled him into the spotlight as one of the most popular NASCAR drivers in history. His popularity has led to huge numbers of collectible items – everything from crystal cars and trading cards to die-cast cars and banks.

Finding these items isn't always easy. Earnhardt has a large and devoted fan base, many of whom are avid collectors of anything featuring his car, image or number. His immense popularity makes some of his merchandise hard to locate, and die-cast manufacturers typically limit the quantities of each item. Even a car that was produced in a quantity of 10,000 pieces may be hard to find. Serious "Intimidator" fans will buy up a limited edition die-cast piece faster than Earnhardt completes a lap at Daytona!

Check the Store

Even if the die-cast version of your favorite Earnhardt car is no longer in production, you may be able to find one if you're willing to do a little searching. That rare car might be closer than you think. Many NASCAR stores stock die-cast cars so may still have pieces after the company stops making them, so be sure to ask retailers if they have what you're looking for. Even if the store does not have it, a retailer might be able to help you find another store that does.

Don't Forget The Races

There are few things more social than a NASCAR race. You find all sorts of people at the nearest speedway, including collectors who might sell or trade cars. Also, retail stores sell die-cast pieces from trailers at NASCAR races, so, the next time you're at a race, keep an eye out for that rare die-cast piece you've been wanting!

Die-Cast On-line

The Internet has become a haven for collectors and NASCAR fans alike. Numerous fans and retailers have set up web sites with NASCAR items in general, and Earnhardt collectibles in particular. Typing "Earnhardt" or "NASCAR" into a search engine will link you to tribute sites, message boards and even on-line clubs where fans and collectors gather and share their admiration for "The Man In Black." Bulletin boards, such as the one at CheckerBee Publishing's web site *(www.CollectorsQuest.com)*, bring like-minded folks together, too.

Internet auction sites are another possibility. Logging on to one of these sites brings up plenty of Earnhardt die-cast products. You can also find other merchandise, such as trading cards and apparel. You just might find someone who has the piece you need to make your collection complete.

Know What You Are Buying

Finding your most coveted die-cast is only half the battle, however. Many of these cars are extremely valuable, so make sure you're getting what you pay for. Familiarize yourself with Earnhardt's driving history. For example, before he landed Wrangler as a sponsor, he had other backers, such as local automotive businesses. The cars based on Earnhardt's early career may be more valuable than the die-cast of his more recent vehicles. And his success with a particular car may also make its die-cast counterpart more valuable, such as the 1998 Goodwrench Monte Carlo in which he won the Daytona 500.

Cars from different years may also vary in value, so learn how they looked over the years. Earnhardt may pick up or drop a few secondary sponsors each year, so for a die-cast car to be authentic, it needs to have the correct decals. The addition of one tiny decal on a Goodwrench Lumina can mean the difference between 1993 and 1994.

Avoiding Wrecks

One of the most important things to keep in mind, especially if you're purchasing die-cast cars via the Internet, is the condition of the car you're buying. Generally, collectors prefer to buy a mint condition car – that is, one that has never been out of the box. However, many collectors want to show off what they have and won't object to taking the cars out and putting them on display. This makes it possible for a car to get a little damaged, and a damaged car in less-than-perfect condition should never be sold for the price of a mint condition car.

Overall, collecting die-cast items is meant to be fun. Trying to find every Earnhardt collectible is a fitting tribute to one of NASCAR'S finest drivers. Just be sure to act fast when you find what you need because, as with Earnhardt's real cars, they're never in one place for very long!

Production, Packaging & Pricing

When you look at a NASCAR vehicle, it's easy to see the intricate creativity that goes into designing such an impressive-looking car. Everything about a stock car, from its modified engine to a special paint scheme, is the result of disciplined artistry and careful planning. In this respect, a die-cast car is very similar to its life size counterpart – just much smaller!

The Body Shop

Since a die-cast car is an artistic representation of a real car, die-cast manufacturers take great pride in their attention to detail. Before production begins, the actual car is photographed from every possible angle so the designers can study every inch. Next, detailed measurements are taken to ensure proper scale. Sophisticated computers are then used to plan the car's color scheme. When the detailing and colors are matched to the real car, designers make a drawing of the die-cast piece, which has to be approved before work continues.

If a design meets standards set by the manufacturer, work can begin on a clay model of the car. Skilled artists hand craft every detail on the model and make it as authentic as possible before they construct a plastic model. After the plastic model is finished, it's time to prepare a mold for the outer shell. A die-cast car's outer shell is constructed of a special zinc alloy, poured into a mold for the car's make and model. Different molds are used to cast the car's plastic components. Once these parts are molded, cleaned and thoroughly inspected, the manufacturers assemble the pieces into a small scale replica of the original car.

True Colors

By all standards, the most important stage of die-cast production is the paint process. In NASCAR, special paint schemes mark the difference between drivers or events. The die-cast car receives a white base coat  then the special color scheme is applied with a serious eye toward authenticity. Sometimes the driver's racing team will supply the manufacturers with paint samples from the actual car so they can get the true colors – not an easy task when re-creating a car as intricate as the Peter Max car!

In the past, some manufacturers placed decals on the die-cast pieces. Today, tampo printing is used to decorate each piece. Logos are rendered by an artist and transferred with a rubber pad onto the die-cast. This is similar to how NASCAR drivers detail their cars.

Parking Space

Since many different companies are responsible for creating die-cast cars, the packaging varies widely. Many of the 1:64 scale cars come in blister packs, although Revell ships some of its small cars in rectangular boxes with windows. Most of the 1:24 cars come packed in protective styrofoam to help prevent damage. Some cars even come in special velvet-lined boxes, ideal for an attractive display.

Making a die-cast replica model of a NASCAR driver's car is a long and meticulous process. It can take months to build one that measures up to the company's standards. But the finished product – complete with a realistic body, authentic paint scheme and real-life detailing – is worth all the effort!

Caring For Your Collection

Although die-cast cars do not require the maintenance that real cars demand, they still need to be kept in good condition if you want to enjoy your collection for years to come.

Left In The Garage

Just as dents or scratches can lessen the value of a real car, flaws in die-cast vehicles can also make them worth less on the secondary market. "Mint condition" pieces not only come with their original packaging, but oftentimes means the piece has never been taken out of its original box. Many packages are specially designed to keep the cars from becoming scratched, dented or marred. Also, a damaged box can also make a piece less valuable, so it's good to keep your boxed collection in a safe, dry place.

Showing Off

Displaying your cars is part of the fun of die-cast collecting. There are ways to keep your cars safe while showing your collection to the world. Display cabinets are available to shield your cars from damaging factors , such as dust or harsh sunlight. You can also buy small plastic boxes designed to house individual cars and keep them safe from damage. Die-cast cars certainly deserve to be displayed and don't have to be kept out of sight.

A Unique Approach

Some die-cast collectors take an interesting approach to acquiring new items – they buy two of the same piece. One item remains in its box to stay in mint condition, and the other is put out on display!

Fan Clubs

NASCAR's popularity has skyrocketed in the past 30 years. The fan base has grown to national proportions, outgrowing the Southeast and encompassing the entire country. And fans make all the difference in the world to such drivers as Dale Earnhardt – a cheering section at a race makes all the sweat and tears worthwhile!

With NASCAR fever at an all-time high, fans from all over the United States can unite to support the sport, cheer for Earnhardt or just collect. No matter what aspect of NASCAR you love, there's a club for you!

Club E

Die-hard Earnhardt fans can support their favorite driver in Club E, the official fan club of "The Man In Black." An annual fee of $19.99 (plus shipping & handling costs) is your passport to the world of Earnhardt racing! In addition to a quarterly newsletter that follows Earnhardt's season and two 1:64 die-cast cars, you'll receive a membership card and a letter from Earnhardt.

The official Club E Photo Cube makes a fine desk ornament. And the Club E Lapel Pin could make wearing a suit all the more bearable, while the sew-on Club E patch adds just the right flair to any shirt. For those out-of-state races, a travel ID tag bearing the Club E logo will help keep your luggage on the right track. And when you get to the race, you can use the three $10 coupons at Action Performance trailers to add to your collection.

Club E
1480 South Hohokam Dr.
Tempe, AZ 85281
1-800-33-CLUB-E
(1-800-332-5823)
www.earnhardtfan.com

NASCAR® Fan Club

If you think NASCAR is too great a sport to be contained in just one driver, the official NASCAR Fan Club might be the right place for you. For an annual fee of $39.99, you can keep up with all NASCAR events via the club's quarterly newsletter. Bonus membership gifts include a personalized membership card and an embroidered hat. An exclusive hood-open die-cast car comes with your membership, too. The first 10,000 charter members each receive a commemorative NASCAR lapel pin.

NASCAR® Fan Club
4707 East Baseline Rd.
Phoenix, AZ 85040
FAX: 1-602-337-3760
www.nascarfanclub.com

Racing Collectables Club of America™

For those who collect racing merchandise, the Racing Collectables Club of America, owned by Action Performance Company, offers a direct line to exclusive die-cast collectibles. A $34.99 lifetime membership entitles you to an official card, an embroidered cap and a subscription to the *RCCA News*.

The Revell Collection Club merged with Action Performance in 1998, so club membership includes access to both Action and Revell die-cast pieces.

Racing Collectables
Club of America™
1480 South Hohokam Dr.
Tempe, AZ 85281
1-800-952-0708
www.goracing.com

Members also have access to the Elite™ and Total View™ series of die-cast cars. Best of all, club members receive $100 worth of travel discount vouchers. You'll be able to go to all those far-away races in style!

Alphabetical Index

COLLECTOR'S
VALUE GUIDE™

Acknowledgements

CheckerBee Publishing extends a special thanks to the many retailers and collectors who contributed their valuable time to assist us with this book, including Jay and JoAnne Badyrka *(FASTRACK, Orange, Conn.)*; Bill Barlow; Bruce Breton and Dave Daniels *(Collectibles of Auto Racing, Pembroke, N.H.)*; Ellie Brinius; Collectible Car Company *(West Chicago, Ill.)*; Chuck Dow; Moe Drapeau; Bill Grey, Violet Posci and Rob Riddell *(Race World, Norwalk, Conn.)*; Emile Lessaird *("Catch The Wave" Emile's NASCAR Connection, Southington, Conn.)*; Tom Flemke Jr.; Tracy Fuhs *(The Race Place, Ottumwa, Iowa)*; Laura Holmes; Serge Kelly; Stephen Lutz; Craig Maraldo; Michael McGreevey *(Prostar 2 Collectibles Inc., Crawfordsville, Ind.)*; Steve Mensales *(Daytona 2000, Daytona Beach, Fla.)*; Cynthia Norton; Don Olson *(Slingshot Racing Collectibles Inc., Deering, N.H.)*; Stanley Pajor *(NASCARDS, Naugautck, Conn.)*; Drew Ridgeway; Dave Rutledge *(Collectables Racing of New England, West Wareham, Mass.)*; Terri Schlesser *(Jerry's Novelties & Collectibles, Le Mars, Iowa)*; Jeff Tamsy *(The Pitshop, Holiday, Fla.)*; Victory Lane *(Newington, Conn.)*; and Wayne Wilkinson.

Catch The Thrill...
with our other hot guides!

CheckerBee
PUBLISHING

NASCAR®
Dale Earnhardt®
Jeff Gordon®
Wrestling
Hot Wheels®
Beer
X-Men®
Fifty State Quarters
Harry Potter™
Ty® Beanie Babies®
Pokémon™

COLLECTOR'S
VALUE GUIDE™

And that's not all! We have 27 great titles available in stores everywhere. They're action-packed! To find out more, call toll free:
800.746.3686 or visit CollectorsQuest.com

It's Racing Excitement

If you're a fan of Dale Earnhardt, our web site is for you! Check it out today!

CollectorsQuest.com

- Keep up with the latest NASCAR news!
- Meet other racing fans on our free Bulletin Board!
- Try your luck with our contest & giveaways!

306 Industrial Park Road   Middletown, CT 06457   800.746.3686   www.CollectorsQuest.com